HEAD FIRST

A RINEHART SUSPENSE NOVEL

A RINEHART SUSPENSE NOVEL

HEAD FIRST

A Yellowthread Street Mystery

WILLIAM MARSHALL

Henry Holt and Company
New York

Published in the United States by
Henry Holt and Company,
521 Fifth Avenue, New York, New York 10175.

Originally published in Great Britain.

Library of Congress Cataloging-in-Publication Data
Marshall, William Leonard, 1944–
Head first.
(A Yellowthread Street Mystery) (A Rinehart Suspense Novel)
I. Title.   II. Series: Marshall, William Leonard,
1944–   . Yellowthread Street Mystery.
PR9619.3.M275H43   1986   823   85-27357

ISBN: 0-03-008034-7

First American Edition

Printed in Great Britain

10 9 8 7 6 5 4 3 2 1

ISBN 0-03-008034-7

The Hong Bay district of Hong Kong is
fictitious as are the people who, for
one reason or another, inhabit it.

SEA-CHANGE

The sea was full of jellyfish. In the moonlight, shimmering, pulsing, opaque circles of light and phosphorescence on the sea, they moved in long meandering armies in towards the harbour on the changing tide. Ahead of the army Hong Kong was a glow of lights in the sky. It nestled between mountains as if it hid in the paws of a kneeling lion. The jellyfish were travelling on the tide and the current straight for it. The jellyfish man, surfacing in the midst of the moving throbbing mass on the surface of the sea, saw the lights of the city and, as he raised his head up to breathe, the lights of the police boat searching for him.

His lungs were on fire. He saw the searchlight from the boat move in a sudden silver circle to his left and begin skimming for him and he ducked down below the surface. He had swum the last fifty yards underwater. He was at the end. In China he had practised and practised holding his breath in a bucket of water, but the bucket of water had not had a patrol boat in it manœuvring in endless circles with a searchlight looking for him. Around his naked ankle he had a rope holding his plastic bag of possessions: all he had in the world and, sinking through the mass of jellyfish, he reached down and hauled it up.

The light passed over him. He had shaved his head in preparation and they had not seen him. He was one of the jellyfish – if there was anything of him to be seen below the bald head it was only a deep shadow.

He could feel the engines of the boat throbbing in the water. During the night he had swum the entire thirty miles across the Pearl River from China out to sea, then, sighting the island, had turned and begun to come in with the jellyfish. The possessions in his plastic bag and the strength he had saved and nurtured and increased over the last year of planning his escape were all he had. He pushed himself up and the throbbing of the engines abated as the boat came about. He sucked in air. He was within a mile of Hong Kong. He saw the lights. In his bag, along with his seven one yuan notes, his talismans and his one piece of lucky jade, he had a scrap of paper with the name of a distant relative in Hong Kong. It was an address in Hong Bay on the southern side of the island. Fearing the unknown, he had swum an extra eight miles to make sure he landed there. For a moment he saw the lights. He saw, he thought, the lights of a truck or a bus on one of the roads along the foreshore. It was dry, bright yellow. Inside the truck there was someone free who lived in Hong Kong going about his business.

He was there. He had made it. Nothing more than another glistening circle on the surface of the sea, he turned and saw the patrol boat as it came about and threw its spotlight on a section of the sea that contained only jellyfish.

His face running with water, wrinkled with the salt, the jellyfish man was crying. His strength and his possessions were all he had left – all he needed to make a life for himself away from the Communists. Silently, he thanked T'ien Hou the goddess of the sea. Each year she sent the jellyfish across the waters of the Pearl River and took them in on her currents to Hong Kong.

He was free. He began breast-stroking through the water and the jellyfish, pushing them gently aside as he slid through their ranks, no longer sickened by their sight and their feel, but part of them, part of T'ien Hou's plan. He was hungry. He had carried no food in his plastic bag for fear of ruining the Chinese paper money that was his fortune and his stake, but he was not weak. He had increased his strength by exercise, not smoked a cigarette for over a year and a half and his body could take everything he asked of it. His resolution was strong and measured. He saw more lights on the roads at the shore of the island and he resisted with ease the urge to celebrate and thrash wildly for the shore. He would arrive with the jellyfish. Like them, like a purified and strengthened man of purpose, he would arrive in time and, in time, with the help of his distant relative and his own strength, he would prosper.

The boat came around and he heard the voice of the European police officer at the searchlight order the helmsman in Cantonese to come around for a wider sweep. Each night they caught refugees swimming from junks or fishing boats or just swimming and they were not going to give up until the morning.

'Come about, Mr Ling!' On the boat, standing by the searchlight, Superintendent Knolls of the Water Police glanced at his watch. It was almost 4.30 a.m., only another hour and a half until the end of the patrol.

'Sir.'

There were jellyfish everywhere – thousands of them. Knolls, looking hard for the poisonous variety, the Portuguese men-of-war with their long dangling tentacles, and seeing none, called to his radio operator, 'Mr Wang, send to station the 4.30 a.m. safety check.' He had no interest in the rights or wrongs of sending illegal refugees back to China. He glanced down at the jellyfish and thought only that if they picked any of them up no one was going to reach down into the sea to help: he or she was going to have to make their own way up onto deck clinging onto the end of a boat-hook. He saw a flurry in the water off to port and called to the lookout amidships, 'Ron? Did you see something then?'

'No.'

He didn't like the things that swam in the South China Sea. Knolls called out, 'It wasn't a bloody shark, was it?'

'Didn't see anything.' Amidships, Inspector Day had a cup of steaming hot coffee in his hand. He also didn't care for what swam in the sea, nor, from the look he gave the radio operator who had made it, what swam in his coffee. Day called out, 'No, sir, I didn't see anything.'

'Two points to starboard . . .'

'Two points, sir . . .'

He was stuck. Something had fouled the rope from his ankle to the plastic bag and he was stuck. The jellyfish man, twisting and arching his body in the sea, reached down to pull at the rope and it was stuck!

'Come around to see what that was anyway . . .'

He was caught. Something had wound itself around the rope of the plastic bag and it was pulling him down and all his strength and practice was for nothing.

'Dead slow . . .'

He felt it. It was something below the surface, down there in the deep, and it was brick heavy and solid, not living, but a reef or a boulder or something in the darkness that had fouled him and was pulling him down.

'At least the bloody jellyfish are going on their way . . .'

They were leaving him, pulsing past: all the jellyfish were going a few inches below the surface, untroubled, and he was going to be left alone in the light. He had come thirty miles – he had practised for a year and a half – he had – he saw the lights of Hong Kong. He saw their warmth and movement. The jellyfish man, shrieking, 'Aii-ya!' wrenched at the rope to free himself.

'*Ron?*'

'I heard it, Boss.'

'All stop!'

He felt it pull him down. Wrenching at the rope, he pulled hard but there was no movement and the knot at his ankle had shrunk in the water and was tight. He felt whatever it was below the surface move, tip. It was a sunken boat or a pipe and it was turning onto its end and beginning to slip off a reef or a ledge into the depths.

'T'ien Hou! Help me!' His head was being pulled down. He was going over backwards. He felt all the muscles in his back and around his spine start to go. 'T'ien Hou! T'ien Hou!'

'YOU OUT THERE IN THE WATER! THIS IS THE POLICE!'

He was going, drowning. His mouth, shrieking to the goddess in supplication, filled with water as he went. He felt the rope around his ankle scrape along something, bounce and rise up and over something. He had a vision of a ship's chain. He looked up and saw the last of the jellyfish pulsing away past him, leaving him, going towards the lights and the distant relative and prosperity as if he had never been part of them or any part of anything. He was dying, drowning. It had all been for –

'He's gone, Boss! I saw him there for a second. He's gone below the water!'

'YOU THERE!' The loudspeaker was useless. There was no one there. Superintendent Knolls called out, 'Mr Ling, steer rudder only in a sweep.' It was 4.30. He looked at his watch.

She was there: T'ien Hou. It rose. Whatever it was holding him, something happened to it and it was released and it rose up. He was going fast. He saw only blackness. He thought for a moment he was dead and he imagined it.

'The bloody sod's drowned!'

He saw them. He was rising and he saw them. Jellyfish. There were more. He saw a second wave of them coming in behind the first. He was rising. Whatever it was beneath him was free and buoyant and it was rising, lifting him up. He felt the plastic bag and the rope come free. He felt air. He saw the lights. He heard . . .

'*There.*'

The boat was almost on top of him.

'YOU THERE IN THE WATER!'

He was crying. He saw the lights. They were calling to him in Cantonese. He felt whatever it was that had held him, in its last cruel joke, push him up and out of the water so they could see him.

'YOU THERE IN THE WATER, THIS IS THE HONG KONG POLICE! YOU ARE – *Jesus*!'

Day, amidships, spilling his coffee onto the deck, said in a gasp, '*God Almighty!*'

'T'ien Hou . . . T'ien Hou . . .' With his face running water he was crying. He felt the hot tears on his face.

'God Almighty, it's a goddamned . . . *coffin*!'

'T'ien Hou . . .'

She listened. The jellyfish had all gone, but she still listened.

5

It was roped closed and all the ropes had come loose.

'Christ in Heaven, it's a bloody Chinese coffin!'

It was. Six foot long and carved in the shape of a single trunk-like shell, the lacquer and varnish glistening on its lid like silver in the light from the boat, it began, slowly, to open.

The jellyfish were all around. Poor, simple creatures, unlike their venomous brothers the Portuguese men-of-war, they had no tentacles. The corpse that drifted out of the coffin had no head.

'T'ien Hou!'

'Forget that bastard and get into the water for the bloody body!' At the searchlight, Superintendent Knolls shouted, 'Mr Ling! Get this bloody boat alongside for Christ's sake and pick that thing up!' He saw the swimmer strike out for the shore. At the controls, Ling was hesitating. Knolls, swinging the searchlight, ordered him, 'For Christ's sake, who cares about one more bloody refugee? Christ, we've really got something this time! Bring the bloody boat alongside *now*!'

'T'ien Hou!' He was shouting his thanks, weeping. He saw the lights and the hope only a mile away in front of him. He saw Hong Kong. He saw freedom.

He heard the boat's engines roar into life.

Not looking back, the jellyfish man, all his life a believer in reward for labour and religious devotion, began swimming for the lights with a certain, hard, unflagging strength.

Hong Kong is an island of some thirty square miles under British administration in the South China Sea facing the Kowloon and New Territories areas of continental China. Kowloon and the New Territories are also British administered surrounded by the Communist Chinese province of Kwantung. The climate is generally sub-tropical, with hot, humid summers and heavy rainfall. The population of Hong Kong and the surrounding areas at any one time, including tourists and visitors, is in excess of five and a half millions. The New Territories are leased from the Chinese. The lease is due to expire in 1997 at which time Hong Kong is due to become a special semi-independent administrative region of the People's

6

Republic with British laws and, somehow, Communist Chinese troops to enforce them.

Hong Bay is on the southern side of the island, and the tourist brochures advise you not to go there after dark.

The corpse was that of a huge, fat man. Dressed in a trailing white linen shroud, without a head, unbalanced and awkwardly turning over and over, it began floating away into the darkness back towards its glistening, empty coffin . . .

I

It was 7.15 a.m.

It was hot.

The air was full of carbon monoxide.

There was smog.

There were people, cars, filth and noise everywhere.

His feet hurt.

And now, to cap it all right off, there was a 6′ 3″ Polynesian leaning against a wall staring at him and wondering why the hell the turbaned, brown-skinned, bearded 6′ 2″ Sikh mailman on Jade Street had blue eyes.

He had blue eyes because something kept going bang inside letter-carriers' letter-carriers and the Hong Kong Letter-Carriers Union, being mainly run by Communists and cop haters, wanted a 6′ 2″ European cop with blue eyes to dress up as a bloody Sikh and carry their letters for them – until he got blown up.

Not only did his feet hurt, but his miniature two-way radio under his beard was heating up the beard glue and the skin dye and making it drip down his neck. Detective Inspector Auden, staring back at the Polynesian, said in a rasp into his unglueing beard, *'He knows I'm not a Sikh!'* There was a burst of static somewhere in the area of the left sideburn. Auden, pausing to sort letters in his hand and trying to look innocent, hissed, 'Spencer! Bill! Can you hear me?' The Polynesian was more than 6′ 3″. He had on a yellow New Guinea T-shirt. He was obviously in disguise. Auden hissed, 'He's looking at the colour of my eyes!' He saw the Polynesian's mitt go into his pants pocket and touch at something there. Auden hissed, 'This is the one! He's the one!' He looked up casually from the letters and glanced across the street without using his eyes. If anyone was going to chuck a bomb into a mail-bag the Polynesian was the one. Auden's .357 magnum was in his desk at the Station. He was unarmed. Auden hissed, '*Bill —!*'

'Put on your sunglasses so he can't see your eyes.'

'I can't. I left them at the Station!' Detective Inspector Spencer was somewhere off on the other side of the street practising being inconspicuous. The practising had worked. He had gone into the realms of the totally invisible. Auden, about to be blown to tripes, hissed into his beard, 'Where the hell are you? I can't see you anywhere!'

'I can see you.' He didn't have to dress up as a bloody Sikh to get down a street unnoticed. Like some sort of Ninja he became part of the place. Auden said, 'He's got his hand in his pocket!'

'Don't look up. Just go on delivering letters.'

'*How the hell can I deliver letters without looking up?*' He heard a whirring sound in the radio. Spencer said, 'I've got him on film.' Spencer said helpfully, 'Ahead of you: three steps to a doorway, up one step, and then the mail-boxes are on your right.' He sounded like the sort of person you could always count on to drop a few coins in your begging bowl. Spencer said anxiously, 'Phil, what's happening? Why are you just standing there?'

Leaving the gun at the Station had been stupid. He could have used it to shoot Spencer's head off. Auden said into his beard with a fixed grin on his face, 'I'm standing here because there's a bloody great Polynesian with his hand clutched around a bomb in his pocket waiting to blow me to bits the moment he sights the blue of my bloody eyes!' Maybe the Polynesian was a bigot. Maybe he only blew up Chinese mailmen. Maybe he —

Spencer was still making the whirring noise through the beard receiver. Spencer said calmly, 'Actually, Phil, no one's been blown up. Whoever does it doesn't actually use explosives. What he does is throw an incendiary device into the mail-bag –'

Oh. That made everything all right.

The beard went whirr, whirr. 'Phil, people are starting to gather.' Spencer said encouragingly, 'You can do it, I know you can. Just move your right foot forward and then . . .'

'*I know how to bloody walk!*'

So did the Polynesian. He took a step forward.

Auden heard the whirring. His last moments were going to be better documented than the Third Reich's. Auden said in a whisper, 'He's –' Auden said, 'I can't move! I can't get my feet to move –!' He heard *whirr, whirr*. Auden, clutching his hand to his beard to turn the volume up on his radio, said in a jammed voice that would have needed twin stereos to make it audible, 'Get over here!' Between him and the mail-sack on his back there was less than an eighth of an inch of leather. Auden, letting go of his beard and pulling at his leg to wrench it up from the sidewalk, said, 'Spencer –!' He looked up and saw the Polynesian looking at him. Auden said, 'Ha . . . !'

The Polynesian said, 'Good morning. John Kamehameha.' He jerked his thumb at the mail-boxes just inside the doorway Auden was never going to reach. The thing he had had in his pocket was his handkerchief. He twisted it anxiously in his hands. He asked, 'Anything for me this morning?'

Auden, not looking down at the letters in his hand, shaking his head, said, 'No.' He went on shaking his head. Auden, shaking, said, for the second time, 'No.' He saw the Polynesian look crestfallen. He was still wringing his handkerchief. Auden was still shaking. Auden, positively, said, 'No. No! Nothing at all!'

'Oh.' The Polynesian turned to go back inside the building and into his lonely, letterless room.

Auden said, 'No.'

He saw the Polynesian's shoulders slump in disappointment.

Auden said, 'Sorry.'

He saw the Polynesian turn on the stairs and nod to him.

Auden called out encouragingly, 'Maybe tomorrow, aye? Maybe tomorrow!'

He had been delivering letters since 5.30 a.m.

It was hot.

His feet hurt.

He heard the camera through his beard radio go whirr, whirr.

Someone, somehow, kept setting fire to letter-carriers' sacks while they were still attached to the letter-carriers' person.

Whirr, whirr . . .

He heard Spencer say happily through the radio, 'OK, Phil? Three steps to the doorway, then one step up, then . . .'

Auden said softly, 'Yeah.'

He began walking.

He turned, saw Spencer poking his head out from behind a mound of packing cases in an alley across the street, and, acknowledging his happy wave, wished only – all the hopes and aspirations of his life rolled into one – that he had thought to bring his gun.

It was 7.22 a.m.

It was hot.

All sorts of people died: Taoists, Christians, Buddhists, Hindus – so on the wall of the waiting-room in the Government Mortuary, in order not to offend, the powers-that-be had hung merely a framed copy of the hours of opening and rules of identification and, the essence of neutrality and tolerance, a Swiss electric clock.

The clock, as silent as the dead in all the rooms around it, read 7.22 a.m. It made not even a click as it passed on and had no second hand to make it conspicuous or an object of concentration.

7.23.

'Deliver us from evil.' Mrs Hwa's words were a whisper. They gave no sound to the silent room. Her hands, on her lap, twisted at a silk scarf and unknotted it. She was sixty-two years old. From peasant Northern Chinese stock, she sat awkwardly on the Swedish tubular steel chair facing the Swiss clock. Her hands were wrinkled and arthritic and her nails, manicured and cared for in the late prosperity of her life, were strong and hard from her childhood, girlhood and early womanhood on the land.

'Chang T'ien Shih, Master of Heaven, deliver us from evil.' She spoke in Hakka, the language of the New Territories farmers. Inside the square of silk she had a silver medallion of Chang T'ien Shih riding a tiger, his demon-brandishing sword held high above him. She touched at it reverently and put it to her forehead.

Somewhere, in one of the silent rooms, beneath another clock that made no sound and had words written on it she did not understand, there was a room with a steel tray and banks of steel instruments and strong lights, and there, all the safety of her family was being examined, inspected, and, as the silent clock watched, making no sound, found to be hollow and wanting.

'Deliver us from evil.'

She thought, for a moment, she heard a sound from one of the other rooms. She thought it was the sound of metal, something sharp and hard and silver, cutting into bone.

In the room she could hear nothing.

'Deliver us from evil!'

The clock in the room made no sound and there was nothing on the wall in front of her but the hours of opening and the rules of identification.

She tried to stand, but her legs and knees had no strength left in them.

She waited, listening, but the waiting-room, planned thoughtfully by the powers-that-be so as not to offend, was completely soundproof and, as the clock and the things it counted continued inexorably and terribly on, she heard no sound at all.

'The subject, Hwa Cheuk Kuen, provisionally identified by a remaining nameplate on the coffin and positively identified by birthmarks and physical peculiarities by a member of the family, was entered on the Arrivals' Register at approximately 5.55 a.m. The coffin in which the subject was received is of Chinese wooden construction bearing marks of a heavy object having been attached to it – possibly a chain – showing signs of forcible entry and considerable water damage from immersion. The subject was partially wrapped in a shroud-like linen material. Signature on Arrivals' documents was Superintendent –' The Government Medical Officer, pressing the Pause button on the tape recorder by the autopsy table for a moment, asked, squinting at the signature, 'Knells?' It seemed an appropriate name.

'Knolls.' Detective Chief Inspector Harry Feiffer, glancing at the silent Swiss wall-clock behind the steel dissecting table, said for the record, 'K-N-O-L-L-S.'

Macarthur, glancing up to the wall, said pleasantly, 'Eerie, isn't it?' He didn't mean the thing on the table or the coffin or the still dripping shroud, he meant the clock. Macarthur said before he pressed again at the tape recorder to continue, 'I was reading the other day that the next thing is going to be whisper-silent electric cranium-saws.' Progress was everywhere. Switching the tape recorder back on with a reassuringly audible click, Macarthur said, 'The subject is a heavily overweight large-boned Chinese male of between 55 and 65, estimated 5' 10½" in height, estimated complete weight 240 pounds, bearing the surgically closed signs of a violent piercing and traumatic series of collision injuries to the upper chest and shoulders.' He even had the death certificate. Macarthur said without having to refer to it, 'Death was caused by a violent penetration of some fixed object entering the area of the heart.' He had seen it before. Macarthur said, not as a question, 'The steering wheel of a car.'

He saw Feiffer glance at his watch.

'Is that the widow outside?' He saw Feiffer nod. 'Death was probably instantaneous, however the subject shows evidence of emergency medical procedures to halt bleeding and needle marks on the left arm where a blood or plasma transfusion line was hastily implanted.' The awful naked thing was on the table in front of him, still dripping water. By it, to one side of him, marking his long white coat with water each time he brushed against it, was the thing's smashed and sodden coffin. 'Emergency procedures appear to have been terminated after a short time when vital signs ceased.' He touched at the sewn wound on the chest with a long, nicotine-stained bony finger,

'The sewing on the wounds has been done quickly so as to clean him up a bit. It doesn't have any medical significance.' Macarthur, with no change in his tone, said for the information of the tape recorder, 'The body is headless.'

It was like some sort of terrible picture of the nightmare men dreamed of in the Middle Ages: a half man, half monster from the outer regions with its face on its chest. It was like some ghastly thing dredged up from the deep – a sodden, rotting, ancient vault opened to disgorge its shredding, disintegrating linen wrapping and exude the smell of old, forgotten, antique death. It was a man on the steel autopsy table. Without its head, its essence, it was some sort of awful, uncatalogued flesh of a sea monster.

It was a man. It was the husband of the woman in the room outside. Once, it had had a voice. Once –

Hwa Cheuk Kuen.

It was a man.

Macarthur said evenly, 'Official lead seals, now broken, on the coffin confirm that the subject, following his death in China, was placed into the accompanying casket in the presence of both Chinese and Hong Kong government representatives and consigned to Hong Kong. There was a small circular chop mark on the underside of the coffin, sighted upon Admission, with the logo of a local coffin repository, confirmed by a fluent Chinese speaker to be –' He looked again at his notes and then up to Feiffer. He turned off the tape recorder.

Feiffer said softly, 'Kan's Western Heaven Coffin Repository, Street of Undertakers, Hong Bay.'

He clicked the button back on, 'Kan's Coffin Repository, Hong Bay.' In the powers-that-be-designed mortuary nothing offended. Macarthur said, 'There is a long, rapidly and roughly done line of stitching at the neck area running laterally from the left collarbone to the right.' He looked up at Feiffer. His voice remained always the same.

Macarthur said evenly, 'The head, judging from the edges of skin protruding as flaps from the stitching – after death – appears to have been surgically removed.'

For some reason, he looked back to the clock.

It made no sound.

'There is a dark stain covering the entire neck and collar-bone area around the stitching that appears to be some sort of chemical compound recently reacted with the sea water in which the coffin was immersed. It is not a bodily fluid.'

She waited. Alone, in the silence, whispering to the talisman in her hand to protect her, Mrs Hwa waited.

Macarthur said softly, 'The compound, in my opinion, is glue. After death, for some reason unconnected with surgical or medical need, the subject's head was removed from his body and the wound closed.'

He saw Feiffer's face. Macarthur said, 'After decapitation, using a form of animal or vegetable glue yet to be established by analysis, an object was then fixed to the shoulders and neck area.' His long fingers reached out and touched at the stains around the neck and flicked at them. The line of glue had spread down over the chest, but through it, there was a clear collar mark where the bulk of it had been applied and held.

Macarthur said softly, 'After death – in China – this man's head was surgically removed and the wound closed, and then –'

He paused.

The clock in the room made a click. It must have been some sort of power surge.

'*Are you telling me they then glued the head back on?*'

It clicked. She heard it. In the room, the silent, neutral, unoffending, unreadable clock clicked.

She heard it.

Macarthur said suddenly, 'No. No, that's not what I'm telling you at all.' He heard the clock click. It was a power surge! It was normality. It was reason. It was the full horror of it all. He touched at the collar mark. 'What I'm telling you is that after he was decapitated – surgically – what they put back on his

16

shoulders was someone else's head. Not his at all. Someone else's head, someone bigger.'

The clock was ticking, making clicking sounds. Like something trying to come alive it was ticking and whirring with the power surge. Macarthur had a cigarette in the top pocket of his white coat. He tried to get it out to put it in his mouth, but his hands were shaking.

'And when the coffin was stolen and broken into – before it was weighed down with chains and sunk in the harbour – that, the bigger, replacement head – that was what was taken.' Macarthur said softly, 'God Almighty, and it was all done in a bloody *hospital*.' He had the cigarette in his mouth but he could not get his lighter to work.

Macarthur said in a gasp in the neutral unoffensive room, 'Jesus Christ Almighty, who in the name of all that's bloody holy could have done something like that?'

She heard it stop. She heard it whirr and break inside and then stop.

The perfect, neutral, Swiss dependable clock. With the surge, it caught, seemed to shake and then, at exactly 7.31 a.m. and 30 seconds, it ceased to be.

'*Deliver us from evil . . .*'

All her talismans were useless.

It had stopped.

Like the rooms all around her, everything encased inside it was dead and gone, extinct and ruined.

'*Deliver us from evil!!*'

There was no one to hear her.

7.31 a.m. and 30 seconds exactly.

Falling to her knees with the medals and talismans on the floor all around her, helplessly, hopelessly, Mrs Hwa began to scream.

2

He had taken up Thoreau. The British took up *Wind In The Willows* or *Winnie The Pooh*, the Chinese took up Confucius, but O'Yee had taken up Thoreau. He was half Chinese on his father's side so he could have taken up Confucius – and on his mother's Irish so he could have taken up inebriation – but since, in Eurasian amalgam, he was a genuine green passport-carrying American, he had decided to take up Thoreau; and whereas his body may have temporarily resided in the Detectives' Room of the Yellowthread Street Police Station, Hong Bay, his soul had decided to remain permanently amidst the bean-fields and leaning hemlocks of Walden Pond.

It happened to you when you reached forty.

'Time is but the stream I go a-fishing in. I drink at it; but while I drink I see the sandy bottom and detect how shallow it is. Its thin current slides away, but eternity remains.' (O'Yee, settling himself at his desk and gazing at the dog-eared page of his copy of the Taipei Intellectual Publishing House's pirate edition of *The Works of Henry David Thoroh* – well, you couldn't have everything for a special price of two dollars fifty – said, nodding, 'Too true.') *'I would drink deeper; fish in the sky, whose bottom is pebbly with stars.'*

Ah . . . It went with being over forty.

The phone on O'Yee's desk rang and O'Yee, still sighing, said, not of this world, 'Yes?'

'D.S.I. C.K. O'Yee?'

It was a woman's voice speaking English. He thought he heard from his little haven the sound of a crinolined nymph calling to him from the acacias.

'Detective Senior Inspector O'Yee, yes.' The initials made him sound like a Bombay Persian carpet factory. He turned a page. Thoreau had had three chairs in his house: one for solitude, two for friendship and three for society. The society chair was out. O'Yee, slipping on his wisdom glasses and regretting his Chinese genes that made it totally impossible for him to grow a long white wisdom beard, asked kindly, 'How may I guide you?' He slipped off his gun and shoulder holster and arranged its straps mystically around his ashtray. O'Yee said softly, 'The mass of men lead lives of quiet desperation.'

There was a long silence.

O'Yee said, 'Hullo, are you still there?'

The voice said softly, 'Christopher.' The voice was Chinese but with a soft Southern twang to it.

O'Yee said, 'Who is this?'

It was definitely a Southern accent. It was someone who had learned English from an impoverished North Carolina teacher of English. It was an improvement on the Chinese who learned it from the impoverished wandering English upper classes. They all went mad trying to affect lisps. O'Yee said, 'Who is this?'

There was another pause. 'A friend.' And another pause, 'This is truly your belief about the mass of mankind?'

It was a bit too early in the morning for philosophical discussions. O'Yee said tersely, 'Look, this is the Yellowthread Street Police Station, Hong Bay. Are you sure you've got the right number?'

'I am becoming sure.' The voice said anxiously, 'I know that you are a man of honesty and self-effacement, a person in a position of power without stain or corruption, a man whose prosperity lies not in the vulgar, cruel accumulation of money at the expense of your neighbour, but one to whom the shining light of truth and probity, above all, is what makes the mark of a man.'

She had obviously checked his credit rating. O'Yee, putting

the book to one side and scratching at his head, said mildly, 'Oh. Um . . . thanks.'

It was a Southern accent. It was the sort of voice that would have old Thoreau eating out of her little, white gloved hand.

O'Yee said, 'Oh, um –' He didn't know what to say.

The voice said softly, musing, 'Hmm.' The voice said evenly, one searcher to another, 'I checked your credit rating.'

The voice said suddenly in harsh, business-like Cantonese, 'Good. I am satisfied.'

The voice said efficiently in Cantonese, 'Do nothing. Hold yourself ready. We are now in total control of the situation.'

The voice said, 'Hmm.' The voice said decisively, 'Goodbye.'

Now the Ninja was a bloody American tourist engaging the Sikh mailman in friendly eyeball-to-eyeball contact for the edification of the folks back home as his small contribution to low profile, non-hostile, international, people-related understanding – essence-wise. Or words to that effect. He had even picked up a flowered shirt from somewhere. Auden, jammed up against a wall, said in a rasp, 'Give me the sunglasses.'

People were passing by. Spencer, taking pictures and going click, click, click, said in his loudest voice, 'Say, can you tell me the way to Jade Street?'

This was Jade Street. Auden said, 'Great, terrific.' He did his best grin, 'Very good.' People were passing all around him. He glanced at them for bombs. Auden said, 'Terrific, you've done it. Now give me the sunglasses I can see hanging on your bloody hibiscus shirt and fuck off.' Auden said in a loud voice, 'My goodness me, I think you are already being in Jade Street.' He was going to add Sahib, but there was a limit. Auden said, 'OK? Now get lost!'

'Say, you're a Sikh person, aren't you?' Spencer said in a whisper, 'They're no good. The lenses are all scratched. They're a pair I found in the car. They're just for show.' Spencer, extending his hand, said loudly, 'William K. Spencer III from Hoboken, New York.' Auden said in a whisper, 'New Jersey!' 'I see that you are one of the few Sikhs I've seen on my *travels with blue eyes. May I ask you a rude question, and enquire if you are a tankaiya, sir?'* Spencer said in an urgent whisper, 'A Sikh who has defected from the faith –!'

People were plotting all over the Colony to set fire to his mail-bag and he was standing there jammed up against a wall – he looked up and saw that it was a four-storey wall full of open windows – talking to a madman. Auden said in a strangled voice, 'Are you out of your fucking mind? Just give me the glasses!'

'They'll fall off!'

'I don't care!' All the Sikhs he had ever seen carried swords or shotguns. Auden, adjusting his turban to make an aerial bomb-deflector out of it, said with murder in his heart, 'Then-go-and-buy-another-pair . . .'

'The shops are closed.' He hadn't taken a picture for a few seconds. He stopped to take a picture. Spencer, speaking through the lens, said, 'Phil, I must have seen about ten thousand people walk by you on your rounds and so far no one has even come close to looking as if they set fire to mail-bags.'

'Maybe that's because –' His ears were ringing. He was hearing Spencer's clicking in stereo. Auden rasped, 'You've got the bloody camera next to your radio transmitter!' It sounded like the final mad rush of an alarm clock before the bomb attached to it went off. Auden, wanting to jump up and down, said, 'What the hell are you trying to do to me?'

'I'm trying to protect you! You haven't even got a gun!' There was a knot of people forming. It was a bus stop. They were waiting for a bus and listening. Spencer, putting down his camera and grinning, said in English – they were all black pyjama-ed Tanka boat people on their way back to their boats after a night on the town – 'Say, I happen to know a little about the mail here in your beautiful Crown Colony of Hong Kong. The first stamps here were issued as far back as 1862 and did you happen to know they were issued in denominations of 96, 2, 18 and 6 cents before they fell into line with the inter-national postal regulations of the equivalent of 30 cents denominations?' That piece of information, if translated into their obscure dialect, would have no doubt made the Tankas' day. Spencer, nodding at them until they looked away, said over his shoulder in a whisper, 'As a matter of fact, that's true. I looked it up in –'

'*Give me the sunglasses.*'

'How will it look if a perfect stranger in the street suddenly hands over –'

'Throw them in the bloody bag!' Auden, clenching his fists and smiling at one of the Tankas who obviously thought someone around here was a little strange, said in awful menace, 'Fairly soon, someone is going to chuck a firebomb from one of the windows above me straight into my bag and as I catch fire, if you are anywhere within hugging distance, I'm going to see that you fry to a crisp right along with me!' He saw Spencer hesitate. Auden said, '*Give me the sunglasses.*' He saw Spencer, defeated, take the glasses from his shirt pocket and drop them into the leather bag on his back. Auden said, 'Thank you! Now you go off, get another bloody disguise and if you see anyone chuck anything into my bag, don't bother running over to help me or do anything useful like shooting them, you just stand across the road like a bloody Quicko-Change-o-bloody expert on the early history of the bloody Hong Kong Post Office and you just bloody *bore* them to death!' He touched at his beard and turban and set them both back in the appropriate places on his head. It was hot. He saw the Tanka boatmen turn around to gaze at him. Yesterday India, tomorrow Hong Kong. Auden, reaching into his bag and taking out the sunglasses and setting them on his nose, said in almost total darkness, 'You know, it was people like him that lost the Empire.' For an instant, as Spencer went back across the street to disappear into the walls again, Auden thought he saw the Polynesian, stoop-shouldered lamenting his absence of mail.

No, it wasn't him.

He thought he smelled, for an instant from his mail-bag smoke.

No, it wasn't smoke.

Auden said softly to himself, 'It's the smell of the pavement starting to melt.'

It was 8.05 a.m.

At last, he was alone and, hidden behind the glasses, safe. Auden said softly to himself, 'Right.' He felt better.

There was a bank of mail-boxes just inside the doorway of the four-storey building and, with the faintest grey whisp of smoke dissipating behind him from his mail-bag as he walked, he went in with new confidence to deliver the mail.

In the vast stone vaults of Kan's Western Heaven Coffin Repository in the Street of Undertakers, Mr Kan said angrily, 'Mr Feiffer, this is Hong Kong, not London or New York!' Outside in the street there was a Chinese funeral going by, all the three bands of gongs and drums, cymbals and trumpets playing at once. He was a small, bald, bird-like man in a blue silk robe. He had to raise his voice to make himself heard. Mr Kan, sweeping his hand around the lines and ranks of tree trunk-like coffins and stone bone-urns everywhere in the place, said, 'Just across the border – a few miles from here – is China where my profession has not changed for ten thousand years!'

The funeral had evidently passed around the corner into Canton Street. The sounds of the bands were abating and there were the shouts and screams of the young white-robed boys at the end of the cortège – the devil-sweepers – scaring off any phantoms of spirit-stealers who might be following the dead man to the cemetery to steal his soul. Mr Kan, standing before the stone bier on which Hwa's coffin had been, said in Cantonese with his voice sharpening, 'There. See there? There, in the corner by the candles and the talismans on the wall, is a bale of hay!' He demanded, 'How long have you lived here in the Colony?'

The smell in the coffin repository was not one of cold clinical death and the stench of water-rotting linen, it was the smell of camphorwood and antiquity. There was no clock in the vaults. Time there was measured in eternities. Feiffer said softly, 'The hay is for thunderstorms. That way, when Lei Kung the evil god comes to steal souls from the dead he will mistake their caskets for haystacks.' Against the far wall, in a candlelit niche, there was a wall painting of a black man riding a tiger. Feiffer said in Cantonese, 'And the coin the black man holds in his hand as he rides the tiger is called Pi Hsieh Ch'ien: flee depravity money – to ward off more evil.' He saw Mr Kan's eyes glittering with anger. Feiffer said evenly, 'No one's blaming you. Have you spoken to Mrs Hwa?'

'She does not blame me.' Mr Kan said. 'Her husband was merely in China visiting relatives. When he died the Chinese – the Communists – did things properly because they are Chinese and I, because I am Chinese, at my end, I also did things properly!' The candles in the wall niches were lightly scented of camphor-wood, like the coffins. Mr Kan said, 'Some things in China, Emperors, Republics or Communist states notwithstanding, *some things do not change!*'

'You didn't open the coffin?'

'*I did not open the coffin.*'

'– to transfer the remains into a family casket?'

'The coffin was sealed with the seals of the People's Republic and the Department of Births, Deaths and Marriages here in Hong Kong!'

'Surely that was merely to clear customs when it entered the Colony?'

'That was merely to clear customs when it entered the Colony.' Mr Kan said, 'All formal, all correct, all very British bureaucratic and Chinese Communist formal – but there was also a personal note from someone at the hospital where the man died saying that for the sake of his family the remains of the deceased should not be viewed!' Mr Kan said, 'A fellow Chinese!' Mr Kan said angrily, 'The coffin was placed here by Mrs Hwa until a propitious time for the burial could be prophesied. Everything here is done correctly – perhaps not according to the Communists or the British who may be temporarily in control of things – but according to the ancient precepts which do not change and will never change!' Mr Kan said, 'Why am I talking to you? You speak Cantonese and your face is understanding and you lay no blame – according to your lights – but everything I say will be put on paper with a typewriter and then I will be judged by people who have no right or understanding to judge me!' As he turned in the candlelight, Feiffer saw he was a very old man. Mr Kan, pointing a bony finger in Feiffer's direction, said, 'Look. See my fingernails? They are the long, uncut nails of a scholar – I know my business. It is not a business at all – it is a vocation! I have been a guardian of the spirits of the dead and the bodies of the dead for over sixty years – since before –'

'The coffin was taken from here and then broken into and dumped in the harbour.'

Mr Kan's hand was trembling. 'As you walked here from the street you came along a crooked path: that was so that ghosts and phantoms who, it is known, can only travel in a straight line could not enter here.' He was blinking, fighting back emotion. 'As you came inside you had to step over a line of stones across the doorway: that was also to keep out spirits – the spirits who can travel a crooked line but who must crawl to do it and therefore cannot climb over a line of stones or rocks.' Everywhere, in niches and on the walls, illuminated by candle-light, there were pictures of The Master Of Heaven and character boards with talismanic prayers inscribed on them. Mr Kan said, 'Hidden away all through this place – unseen – there are pieces of jade and fern and ginger, scraps of the fur of dogs, and, set into every plinth on which a coffin rests or in every niche where a bone-urn awaits reburial, there are silver coffin nails blessed by a Taoist priest. Look there!' He pointed upwards to the stone lintel above the doorway of the vault, where, in sprigs, there were willow swords and mugwort and aromatic plants – all defences against demons. Mr Kan, seeing Feiffer looking instead at his face, demanded, 'Look!'

'I understand all that.' Feiffer, reaching out to touch the man's robe, said quietly, 'You cannot be held responsible for what happened.' He had thought briefly that there might have been fingerprints on the plinth where the coffin had stood, but, like everything else in the room, it was covered in a thin film of undisturbed dust and candle-soot. Feiffer said quietly, 'Something terrible has happened and the body is no longer entire.' It was the worst fear of the Chinese, dismemberment after death. Feiffer said, 'It is extremely important that we find out who took the body and why.'

'I can tell you nothing! I did everything that the ancient laws and traditions demand I do and I did nothing wrong according to any Chinese who understands such things!' Mr Kan said desperately, 'What you will put in your typewritten report will make no difference to me because the things that you will find important no Chinese would ever find important.' Mr Kan, in tears, said hopelessly, 'Anyone – anyone – could have come in here at night and done what he liked!' It was hopeless. It would all be typewritten in English, mulled over by Europeans, and not understood at all. Mr Kan, shaking his head, said, 'Everything, everything I have done in here – the trouble I have gone to, willingly – was – was for – solely, *celestial* security!'

In the vault, throughout the entire establishment itself, there was not one lockable door.

'I cannot understand!' Mr Kan, tears rolling down his cheeks, the guardian of ten thousand years, shaking his head, said hopelessly, 'I cannot understand. I simply cannot understand how this could have happened or why!'

His own coffin – ready for him for the last thirty years and polished daily to a sheen – was by the vacant plinth where Hwa's casket had rested and, still shaking his head, he went soundlessly across to it and stood staring down at it in silence.

She might have had his number, but after careful consideration, the brain nurtured on the slow, deep logic of Thoreau, had hers.

On the phone in the Detectives' Room, O'Yee, leaning back in his chair and playing with a pencil, said in Cantonese, 'Ah, it's you again.'

Chinese was better than English. It had the weight of a bigger birth-rate behind it. O'Yee said, 'Does my credit status show me to be a man of poor but honest nature or, merely, does it show me to be a soul of venality who hoards his gold secretly beneath the cherry tree in his garden?' He thought that sounded deep. O'Yee said, 'Your accent in English shows you have been taught by a Southern Baptist.' She was a goddamned Jehovah's Witness who had got his name out of the phone book. O'Yee, waiting for the gasp of surprise, said in English, 'Sorry, not today thank you.' He waited for her to call him 'Friend'. (Or was that the Quakers?)

'We are pleased that you are critical.' She was still speaking in English.

He waited for her to call him 'Brother'.

'– Miss Fan.'

O'Yee said, 'Pardon?'

'My name is Miss Fan.'

'You represent the ministry – right?'

'Yes.' Miss Fan said, 'Yes.' She sounded pleased. (They all did.) Miss Fan said, pleased, 'I represent the Ministry.'

'Which particular one?' O'Yee's voice said silently, 'As if I didn't know.' He did. They all talked that way. It was the Mormons.

Miss Fan said intimately, 'Mr O'Yee. . . .'

O'Yee said, 'Hmm?'

Miss Fan said, 'Christopher . . .' She seemed to be deciding.

O'Yee said, 'Uh huh . . .' O'Yee said, 'Which particular ministry do you belong to?'

Miss Fan said, 'The Ministry of External Calm. The MEC.'

He waited.

Friend –

Brother –

Acolyte?

Pal?

Miss Fan said, deciding, welcoming him to their ranks, '*Comrade*.'

'Spencer.' The radio was making fizzing noises in his beard. 'Spencer!' No, it wasn't the radio making fizzing noises in his beard, it was the mail-bag making fizzing noises on his back. Auden in the corridor of the filthy four-storey slum building with his hand stuck in a letter slot, yelled at the top of his lungs, 'Bill! Bill! Where the hell are you?'

He was gone, he was invisible, he had evaporated. Auden, smelling smoke, seeing smoke, wrenching at his fingers and getting them caught even tighter, twisting, turning, trying to get to the bag with his free hand, shrieked in not a Sikh voice, but in a totally unintelligible yell of a man about to be set fire to, 'BillforChrist'ssakegethereandhelpmeI'mstuckinaletter-boxand – I'm bloodywell *on fire!*'

He wasn't on fire. Yet. He was merely smouldering preparatory to being on fire. Auden, twisting, grabbing for the bag and getting only grey smoke in his hand, shrieked, 'Bill! Bill! Where are you?'

'Phil! Gzzumph!' He heard it in his beard. Auden yelled into the whiskers, 'Where the hell are you?'

'Gzzumph . . . film for my camera. . .' The radio cleared for a moment and Spencer asked calmly, 'What seems to be the trouble?'

'I'mburning! Thebag'ssmokingandI'mstuckinabloody −'

Spencer's voice said calmly, 'Is there someone there? Do you want me to take a picture?' There was a whirring sound and then Spencer's voice said apologetically, 'I ran out of film. I'm just in the next street where there's an early-opening camera shop.' Spencer said with a trace of annoyance in his voice, 'Phil, I can't carry on a long conversation with you by radio or they'll think I'm in here looking for porno photos or something.'

'Bagonfire!'

'What?'

'The fucking bag's on fire! THE FUCKING BAG'S ON FIRE!'

'Take it off!'

'I can't take it off! I've got my hand stuck in a letter slot!' He knew what he was going to ask. Auden shouted, 'I got my hand stuck in a fucking letter slot when the fucking bag started smoking!'

If it was a porno photo shop they must have felt at home with the prose. Spencer, still making whirring noises across the ether, said urgently, 'I'll get to you. Where are you?'

'I don't know where I am! I'm in the corridor of a building!'

'Give me the exact address!'

'I don't know the exact address!'

'Well . . .' Maybe it wasn't the camera making whirring noises, maybe it was Spencer's brain. He was thinking fast. Spencer said, 'Right! To find the right address −' He had it. Spencer said, 'Quick, look at the address on the topmost letter in your bag!'

Imminent death brought a wonderful tranquillity of mind. It was the people left behind who had to be considered. Auden, considering one of them, said pleasantly, 'Oh, good idea, Bill, well done.' No point in making your last words abusive. Auden said, 'The only small difficulty about that, Bill, appears to be that my bag – you know, the bag holding the topmost letter – just seems to be slightly on fire . . .' There was a whoomph from some unimportant area of his body like his spine. Auden said evenly, 'No, I shouldn't die with a lie on my lips – it's *completely* on fucking fire!

He saw flames. Inside the bag, all the letters were burning. Next it would be the leather bag and then, next –

Auden, bashing, rubbing, thumping his bag hard against the bank of letter slots in the corridor, wondering where the hell he was, shrieked as he smothered in smoke, 'Spencer! Spencer! Get over here and if I'm still able to pull a trigger when I see you, send for my fucking *gun*!'

He was wrong. In the autopsy room of the mortuary, Macarthur, glancing up from Hwa's body to the stopped clock, shook his head.

He had been wrong. Lying on top of the headless thing's chest he had a text book of Chinese surgical practice and, looking at the photographs and diagrams of the sort of suturing they did there and comparing it with the rough stitches around the flap of skin where the decapitation had been closed up around the neck, he had been wrong.

He had thought the unfamiliar sutures had been the work of a surgeon in China, done roughly and quickly and post-mortem in line with an alien practice about which, in Hong Kong, he knew little.

They weren't. The suturing method recommended there, laid down, insisted upon by the manual of practice, was the same as that done in every hospital all over the world.

He leaned down and peered at the line of stitches where the neck had been.

He had been wrong.

Whoever had taken the head and closed the wound, like a surgeon had done the procedure a thousand times. But not as a surgeon.

He had been wrong.

On the steel table in front of him, was not the headless body of a man at all – at least not to the mind of the man who had done it. What he had in front of him was a carcass and the man who had worked on it had not been a surgeon at all, but something totally different again.

He had been a *butcher*.

It was a little after 9.32 a.m. on a hot, hazy day.

In the New Hong Bay Cemetery on Aberdeen Street, the Resurrection Squad, six fit young Chinese in coveralls and caps, holding picks and shovels, waited behind a tree for the finish of the poor man's three-band funeral on the north side of the grounds so they could work at a grave in the old section undisturbed.

Under their coveralls they each carried Browning Hi-Power automatic pistols. From time to time, one or other of them touched at the bulge the weapon made to check it was still there and ready.

There was no hurry.

The Resurrection Squad, ready to dig, waited patiently.

3

'What the hell's going on, Harry?' John Yin of The Society For Neglected Bones, staring hard at the high-walled Army-style tent that screened off grave number 4567/98 in his records from the rest of the old section of the cemetery, said in his perfect Harvard Business School English, 'On behalf of the Society – as its secretary – I have to register a protest. I do register a protest.' They all stood together on a little hillock overlooking the harbour. At the tent there were cars and pick-up trucks loaded with shovels and what looked like mechanical diggers. He saw Constables Lee and Sun on guard at the trucks gazing into their cabs with a mixture of horror and interest on their faces. God only knew what was in the front of the trucks. In his full-time job Yin was in real estate. In his part-time position as secretary of The Society For Neglected Bones, presumably so were his clients. Yin said urgently, 'In the Society it's our job to keep an eye on the remains of people whose relatives might have neglected their graves – we expect police interest in cases of vandalism, but this is ridiculous!' He was well dressed in a light fawn suit. Standing next to him, Feiffer's own stained white suit contrasted badly with it. Yin said, 'The cemetery keeper said all he did was report a patch of recently dug-up ground on the grave – it's probably just a dead cat someone wanted to get rid of!'

It was a still, hot day, at 10.10 a.m. getting hotter. Inside the canvas tent there was no sound at all.

Feiffer said, 'Ping Kit-Ling – Kitty Ping, is that who's buried here?'

'Yes! Like a lot of people without relatives she entrusted her grave care to us.' He had a small hand-written scroll in a lacquered roll-case in his pocket given to him by the cemetery keeper. He unrolled it quickly and read the cursive style the Society used for its records, 'She was a 69-year-old widow from off Empress Of India Street.' Yin, hearing a scraping sound from behind the tent, said, horrified, 'They're digging her up in there, aren't they?'

'The Government Medical Officer, Doctor Macarthur –'

'Bullshit!' Yin, lowering his voice so the two Chinese constables could not hear, said in a whisper, 'They're digging her up in there, aren't they?'

'Yes.'

'Why?'

'I can't tell you why.'

'You need an exhumation order! The fact that ground has been disturbed doesn't give you probable cause for –'

'The order was issued in Judge's Chambers an hour ago.'

'On whose authority?'

'On mine.' Feiffer, looking away from the tent, looked down at the cursive script on the scroll in Yin's hand. Both the scroll and the hand that held it had been created with care. The manicured nails alone would have cost more than Feiffer paid for his haircuts. Feiffer said, 'The best I can do is give the Society a watching brief on the proceedings from outside.'

'Why? How? On whose authority? *On what basis?*' Yin, forgetting Harvard, his expensive suit, his manicured nails and his English, becoming in a moment the Secretary of the most ancient co-operative society on the face of the earth, and Chinese, said in rapid Cantonese, 'We guaranteed her rest and – *Have you any idea what you're doing according to my – and her religion?'*

From behind the tent, or below it, or wherever Macarthur and his helpers from the Department Of Public Works actually were in the tomb, there was a series of hard, metal on metal sounds. At the trucks, the two Chinese constables Lee and Sun, looking uncomfortable, moved away. Feiffer said, 'Yes. We do know what we're doing.' In the grave, if he was right, all the damage had already been done. Feiffer said softly in English, 'I'm sorry.' He saw Yin shake his head. His English, like his patience, was gone. Feiffer said in Cantonese, 'She died in China, didn't she?'

'All the more reason to respect her Chinese religion!' Yin, shaking his head, said, staring at the tent and speaking so softly Feiffer had to crane to him to hear him, 'She wanted to make a final visit to Honan province where she was born and –' He heard the metal on metal sound turn into unmistakable digging. Yin said suddenly, 'You can stop this! All you have to do is say the word and you can stop this!' He saw Feiffer shake his head, 'Harry, you can stop this!'

'No.'

'I want to be present! I want to be present when the coffin is opened and I want someone with a camera from the Society to record everything that happens and make sure that everything –' He had gone into the Society as a stepping-stone in his business: to make sure that the real estate of cemeteries was not disturbed for building blocks, or, if it was, that it was his company that disturbed it. Yin, moving back and forth from one foot to the other, forming his hands into fists, said in English, 'I have a right to be present!' After Harvard, he had always thought of himself as an urbane, world-weary atheist. He wasn't. There, staring at the tent, hearing the sounds, he was who he was. John Yin – Yin Ju-tai – said in desperate Cantonese, *'Harry, what in the name of heaven is happening here?'* From behind the tent walls there was a crack as they broke into the coffin with an axe or a hammer or the gods only knew what. Yin said, 'Harry, please! Please, I ask you as a friend – as someone who's known you and your family for – Harry, please – *don't let this happen!'*

'It won't reflect on you. No one will know.'

'*I don't care if it reflects on me!* All I care about –' He heard a thump. Behind the tent they had the coffin open and someone wearing rubber soles had got down onto the lid. He closed his eyes and saw pictures he did not want to see. Yin, looking away to the harbour and the horizon and finding no comfort there, said brokenly, 'Harry, please . . .'

'It's open!' It was Macarthur's voice. It came from behind the walls of the tent, from somewhere in the ground.

He had the scroll in his left hand. All the writing, all the records and promises of eternity, were all written in a careful cursive calligraphy in indelible ink. Yin said softly, 'Please, Harry . . .' He looked hard at the two Chinese constables by the trucks. He saw them look away. Yin said in Cantonese as Feiffer touched him on the shoulder to anchor him in place as he himself went forward towards the tent, 'She was a harmless, sad, lonely old woman who –'

Yin said in final entreaty, in English, 'She's been in the ground there for over thirteen months! She hasn't got anybody left in the world to protect her! Please! Please, *couldn't you just leave her alone?*'

In the hole behind the tent the coffin was open. For an instant he smelled it. He saw the two Chinese constables look at him helplessly. Feiffer was at the entrance to the tent. He saw him pause for a second to steel himself, then glance back before he ducked down to go inside.

There was no wind. From the hillock at the northern end of the old section of the New Hong Bay Cemetery overlooking the harbour, he could see only the sea and the horizon. He had the timeless, indestructible scroll in his hand.

Yin, crushing it hard in his fist, pressing so hard that he felt his manicured nails draw blood from his palm, said with his Harvard education, his perfect, learned, practised, honed English all leading to this one moment, 'You dirty, stupid, unthinking bastards! Everything – everything Chinese – everything it means or ever did mean – everything in heaven or earth – everything made her believe our promise to her that nothing like this would ever happen!'

On the phone, Miss Fan said simply, 'Contact me. Important.'

It was the Moonies: that was what the Ministry Of External Calm was these days – it was the Moonies.

O'Yee, nodding his head, holding his pirate edition of Thoreau up in front of him as a shield, said definitely, 'You're the Moonies, aren't you? That's who you are.' He had been through the Classifieds in the phone book three times and rung

34

New Numbers twice and found nothing. O'Yee said, 'Right. I'm right, aren't I?'

There was a pause.

O'Yee said, 'Sorry, I'm a Catholic.' That always seemed to work on people who knocked on your door telling you that they had just knocked on your soul.

There was another pause.

Maybe most of the Moonies were drawn from Catholics.

Miss Fan said again, 'Contact me.'

'A nominal Catholic with a strong, independent, enquiring mind.'

'Contact me. Find me.' There was a brief silence. Miss Fan said, 'Important.'

She hung up.

In the tent, they had a gas lantern hung a little way down into the hole above the open coffin. The awful smell of corruption and rotting linen and ancient death was coming from down there. There was almost no room in the tent with Macarthur and the two diggers from the Department Of Public Works, and no other smell but the smell coming upwards on the hot air of the lantern.

He looked down into the hole.

There was no lid to the coffin. It lay to one side in the hole, dripping moisture, the split and broken grain in its wood picked out by the bright white light.

He smelled it.

He looked down into the hole.

Feiffer said in a whisper, 'Oh my God –'

For an instant, he had to close his eyes before he looked again.

In the tent, there was only the gentle fizzing of the lamp.

Feiffer said again, softly, 'Oh my God . . . !'

In the central sorting room of the Hong Bay post office on Great Shanghai Road, Auden was still wringing wet from the fire bucket Spencer had emptied over him in the corridor of the four-storey building on Jade Street. It had been a very small corridor and a very large bucket. Auden, standing over a trash

35

bin and squeezing out what looked like the last drops of vital bodily fluid from what looked like a dead beaver, his false beard – said in a snarl to the dead-letter man, 'I can't do this in the rest-rooms, can I?' He couldn't do it in the rest-rooms because the entire sorting office and mail-delivering staff was on strike in the rest-rooms playing cards. Auden, squeezing, throttling, said with a nod, 'Right?'

'*Ngoh m'sik. Ngoh m'sik gong Ying-gwok wa.*'

Oh, yes he did. He spoke bloody English all right. As well as being the Dead-Letter Man and the bloody Rest-Room Man he was also the Post Office Union Man – and a goddamned Communist. He was a small, weedy-looking Southern Chinese wearing rimless Goebbels glasses. Auden said with a smile, 'Why can't I use the rest-rooms? Afraid I might find an illegal gambling game going on in there?' As he wrung, he squelched. Auden, glancing at Spencer, said with the same fixed smile, 'If you'd given me another few seconds I could have got the fire out by myself.'

The dead-letter man said in an undertone, 'Oppressors of the working class.'

Auden said, 'What? What was that?'

'It hurts to do an honest day's work, doesn't it?' The dead-letter man said, 'Look at this mess you've left me!' He had the contents of Auden's mail-sack spread out on a table next to Spencer's camera, Spencer's collection of useless Polaroid photos showing nothing and – more tantalizingly – Spencer's gun. The dead-letter man, reaching into the depths of the letter sack and fishing out a wad of soggy, charred letters, said, 'It's our job to see that the mails get through.'

'People are blowing up mail-bags!'

'Then it's your job to see they don't blow up mail-bags so we can do our job and get the mails through.' He was still fishing. He came out with an Hawaiian postcard with stuck-on yellow sand showing the beach at Waikiki at sunset. He held it up to show Auden what the true capitalist workers' hell looked like. The dead-letter man said, 'This address doesn't even exist. You should have checked all the addresses before you went out so you wouldn't have to bring things like this back undelivered.'

He put the postcard in the pocket of his apron. He saw Spencer looking sympathetic. The dead-letter man said, 'And you, you're supposed to catch the person who is responsible for all this destruction and clap him into a dungeon!' For someone who didn't speak English he was doing all right. The dead-letter man, looking suddenly guilty, said, 'I-speak-a-little-English.'

Auden said with the same fixed smile, 'I think it's you. I think the Chinese are about to take over the Colony and in order to curry a little favour with them you've been putting little bombs in with the mail and blowing up your own postmen.' His turban was also on the table. It also was wringing wet. The colour in it was running. Auden, taking it up and making a garrotte out of it in his hands, said menacingly, 'I think it's your little blow against the capitalist system, so you and all your mates can go on strike and sit around in the crappers playing cards and making money.'

'Phil, we checked all the mail under the X-ray equipment.' The garrotte wasn't quite right. At least Auden knew something about being a Sikh. He put a knot into it and turned it into a thuggee's strangling cloth. Spencer, going forward and putting his hand on Auden's shoulder (and relieving him of the noose), said solicitously to the dead-letter man, 'No one's accusing you of being a Communist.'

The dead-letter man said, 'I am a Communist.'

'Then why the hell do you work for the bloody Government?' He had found it – the clue. Auden said, 'Ah!' If postmen were getting set fire to, and there was no one following the postmen around setting fire to them, and all the mail had been checked by the cops and the dead-letter man, and you could be sure it wasn't the cops because it was one of the poor bloody cops who had to be a bloody Sikh mailman and get set fire to, then you could be pretty sure that it was the dead-letter man who was doing it. He paused, thinking. It was too deep a thought to put into a simple sentence, but it was all there. Cherchez la Red. Auden, advancing, said –

'Phil, I think it was my fault.' Spencer, still touching him on the arm, patting him, smiling, said, 'No, it was all my fault.' (Auden didn't argue.) He looked at the dead-letter man, 'Look, we mustn't all fall out over this.' There were soggy letters everywhere, 'After all, the mail must get through.'

Auden said, 'Why?'

'Because the poor, ordinary working people of this imperialist-dominated post-Empire colony need to be told the true facts about the world from the letters they receive from the glorious People's Republic!' The dead-letter man said, 'You can't use the rest-rooms because you're not an employee!'

'No one's throwing things into the bloody mail-bags! The only person who threw anything into my mail-bag was bloody *him*!' He saw Spencer look surprised. 'And that was just a pair of bloody sunglasses that the bloody Post Office should have supplied anyway if I was one of their standard bloody Sikh mailmen!'

The dead-letter man said, 'We don't have any Sikh mailmen. If we did we would have supplied sunglasses.'

Auden said, 'I'm not going out there again with another bloody load of letters to get blown up again and be driven mad by him!' He was squelching. It was getting to him. Auden, picking up his beard and taking his turban back from Spencer, said in desperation, 'I'm wet! Look at me! I'm all bloody *wet*!'

His English, when it came to it, wasn't all that bad at all. The dead-letter man, looking him up and down, said quietly, 'Right. Yeah.' He too, now, was smiling. The dead-letter man said quietly, 'Oh, brutal guardian of unfair laws and repressive legislation, without your uniform and your gun, isn't that the truth?'

She had been in the ground for over thirteen months. Once, the face that looked up at him from the rotten linen and cracking wood of the coffin had been a human face. It had been Ping Kit-Ling, a person. At the coffin, to one side of it in the ground, *in* it, Macarthur, pulling back the shroud, called up, 'Stitches. Sutures.' It had been cut, dismembered. It was the worst fear of the Chinese: it had gone into the ground not whole. The stench and the sight of what looked like old rotting cobwebs about her face was awful. Macarthur called up, *'Glue.'* All the hair on the head was gone and Feiffer could see bone glistening in the lantern light. Macarthur called up, 'Just like the other one.'

He was bending over the awful object. It was as if, to him, it had no smell at all. Macarthur, touching at the top pocket of his long white coat for something and not finding it, called up, 'I can't find the notes I made. Where did this one die?'

Feiffer said, 'Honan.' His voice sounded strangled. He saw Macarthur look up and put his hand to his ear. Feiffer said louder, 'She died in Honan province in China.'

'Right.' It all was merely what he did. Macarthur, leaning across the ruined creature and pulling at the side of the coffin to lift it up, said, 'You can see here where they smashed open the lid and here –' He bumped the object in the coffin with his elbow and seemed almost to say 'Excuse me'. 'Here you can see the seals of the Chinese government and the seals of the Hong Kong Births, Deaths and Marriages people.' He called up, 'This confirms it. These aren't the sutures of a surgeon – they're a butcher's carcass stitches, but what the most fascinating aspect of it all is –' He moved back and got himself a better purchase on the sides of the coffin. 'Is this.' He wrenched the shroud back and, indicating where the entire chest had been – where there was now nothing – Macarthur said, 'Look! Look at these marks on the floor of the coffin – the body outline.'

He glanced up and saw Feiffer with his hand to his eyes.

Macarthur said, 'They dug her up and took away the chest that had been glued on, but look, look at this – look at the really strange thing.'

Macarthur said, 'Look at the outline of the body symmetry. Look at the line of her shoulders and then her hips and legs.' He had the whole naked, rotting thing exposed.

Macarthur said, shaking his head, fascinated, 'Harry, the chest that they glued on this woman's body when it was still in China – after they'd cut her in three – look at the line of depression in the coffin floor where the weight has been – it wasn't her chest at all!'

That was what they had come for. Whoever, in the last few hours had dug her up, that was what they had come for and taken.

Macarthur said, 'It was a man's chest. Look at the difference in symmetry and the extra weight. It wasn't her chest at all they glued back on. *It was the chest of a man.*'

He called up, fascinated, 'Harry, drop the light a bit lower, would you? Maybe you'd like to take a closer look yourself . . .'

'Christopher, I wish you wouldn't keep doing this to me . . .' On the phone, Father MacSweeney of the Irish Columban Missionary Fathers to the Far East, said in his lilting Cork accent, ' 'Twasn't enough that at dinner with you and Emily and the children last week, I had to be the expert who told young Patrick all about the Spanish Inquisition for his class history paper, now you're rubbing salt into the wound by testing my urbanity.' He paused. He was smiling. He was always smiling. At the seminary in Ireland he had smiled so much and been so unruffled that, in the end, he had paid one of the second-year men money to hit him in order to make him mad. At the end of the beating he was still smiling. Father MacSweeney said, 'The MEC, is it?'

'Yes.' O'Yee had the door to the Detectives' Room closed. O'Yee said, 'The Ministry Of External Calm.' To get a hard answer out of the Father you had to put it in dire terms. O'Yee said, 'They're soliciting for my soul.'

'God help them then.' He thought he heard MacSweeney laugh. 'No, I stand corrected. God wouldn't help them.'

'It's the Moonies.' O'Yee said, 'It's the Moonies – isn't it?'

MacSweeney said, 'Ha, ha, ha, ha.' Even when he laughed at you he was still smiling. O'Yee could see why the second-year man had accepted the offer to beat him up. MacSweeney said, 'Christopher, I've been reading my Thoreau too, after you told me that salvation lay not in religion but in solitude, and do you know that man talks of nothing else but avoiding giving dinner and conversation to his fellow man on one page, and then the delights of getting dinner from his fellow man on the other?' The only rock was that of the Holy Mother Church. MacSweeney said, 'All this enquiry, you know . . .' MacSweeney said, 'The Ministry Of External Calm after your immortal soul . . .' He said, 'Good man yourself, Christopher, that's a rich one!' He said, 'Ha, ha, ha!' He asked, 'Isn't it about time we saw you at Mass?'

He said, always full of hope and joy and optimism, and

therefore an unending trial to his friends, 'Sure, the Ministry Of External Calm is the Chinese Secret Service. You know, like the KGB – only worse. Surely you knew that?' He said, laughing, 'The Spanish Inquisition, Henry David Thoreau, the Ministry Of External Calm . . . what will it be tomorrow? Tibetan prayer wheel translations?' He said happily, 'Ha, ha, ha!'

He said anxiously into the sudden terrible silence on the line, 'Hullo, Christopher . . . Are you still there?'

'Get it out of there! Put the goddamned lid back on it and get a goddamned rope and get it out of there!' He knew John Yin heard. He knew not even the two uniformed men by the trucks would be able to stop him coming in. He knew they wouldn't even try. 'Get it up and get it out of there!'

She was in bits. Like some sort of awful, ghastly, rotting, soulless unhuman object, she had been taken apart and put back together and violated, robbed, thrown aside as if all her life had been nothing more than a –

He heard Yin coming. He heard his footfalls on the ground as he ran. In the open grave where she lay in bits – where the stench and odour overwhelmed him – the lantern was swinging backwards and forwards as Macarthur bent over her, picking at her, studying her, examining her.

He heard Yin come. In his hand he would have his scroll and his promises.

She was in bits. She was –

Feiffer, seeing one of the Public Works men at the flap to the tent about to flee, yelled in Cantonese, 'You! Do your bloody job here and get the bloody lid back on the coffin and get it all out of here and –' He saw Yin at the door, his eyes wide with horror.

'*What have you done?*'

'John . . .'

He had forgotten all his English. He fought to get in as Feiffer, blocking his way, held him back at the open flap to the tent.

He smelled it.

He saw Feiffer's face.

In the Cantonese of his ancestors, of the souls of people his society had protected and had promised to protect for ten thousand years, John Yin, on the verge of hysteria, shouted at the top of his voice, 'You bastards! You vandals! You *foreigners*! *What have you done!?*'

4

On the phone, the Commander said very calmly and evenly, 'Harry, are you telling me that somewhere – somewhere in that bloody cesspit of iniquity and chicanery you police, there's someone running backwards and forwards with bits and pieces of human bodies to a little room wired up like a 1930s RKO serial, building a bloody improvised *monster*?' There was a pause. 'You had better not be telling me that. What you had better be telling me is that some bright spark's found a bigger and better way to smuggle heroin in from China, or you had better be telling me that it's a case of substituted bodies to cover up a perfectly ordinary, run-of-the-mill domestic murder or a –' He ran out of possibilities. 'But you had better not be telling me that bodies are coming in from the People's Republic of China with mismatched bits glued on and that someone's digging them up and taking them away!' He waited, but there was no reply. The Commander said, 'Well? I'm waiting for a perfectly rational, ordinary, sensible, mundane, pedestrian answer!'

'I haven't got one. I'm simply telling you what I know.' He was on the car radio, patched into the Commander's phone. Across at the hillock, hidden behind the tent, Macarthur and the men from the Department of Public Works were getting the coffin out of the ground to load it into the morgue van. Feiffer said, looking away from the scene, 'I don't have any suggestions, mundane, pedestrian or otherwise to offer you.'

'There are plenty of recorded cases of smugglers secreting diamonds or drugs or God knows what in the stomachs of corpses.'

'There aren't too many of them where they secret it in the head.' Feiffer said evenly, 'And usually they use the stomach the corpse has already got. They don't get someone to slice it into bits so they can glue on another.'

'A surgeon —'

'Macarthur says, "a butcher".' At the other end of the line there was what sounded like the sudden intake of breath preparatory to an explosion. Feiffer said quietly, 'Look, Neal, all I can tell you is what I've found, and what I've found is the body of a 65-year-old male Chinese in a coffin in the bay, with no head and evidence that the head that he did have wasn't his, and, secondly, the body of an elderly Chinese female in a grave in Hong Bay, with no chest and evidence that —'

'That someone in China — after she was dead — removed her chest, sewed up the wounds, and, before or after she was placed in a coffin to be sent back to Hong Kong, glued the chest of a man to her!' The Commander said suddenly, 'Harry, have you any idea what's been happening in the last few months? Have you stopped to read the papers or catch the end of the news or just —' His calm was going. The Commander said as to an idiot boy, 'The lease on this Colony runs out in a few years and for the last few months the British, the Chinese, the local businessmen, the Governor — in fact, everybody — has been busily negotiating with the Communists so that when the changeover comes it might be peaceful and not be the greatest exercise in riot since the bloody Crusades!' It had been settled only in the last ten days. The Commander said, 'Finally, finally, it's been settled that the Colony can go on another fifty years in its present form and everyone, including the Chinese, have been expending their energies in convincing the local population, who are not in love with the Communists, that the Communists can be trusted to keep their word — and now you're telling me that in China, people from Hong Kong are being cut up in their coffins and used as — as what? As spare parts for something out of bloody *Coma*?'

'No one has suggested it's some sort of government enterprise.'

'Then what is it?' The Commander said, 'There isn't a lot of scope for private spare-part surgery in China – it's a Socialist republic! You know, where the bloody government pays from the cradle to the grave!' Something occurred to him. 'Coffins that come in from China are sealed by the Chinese and by a representative from the Department of Births, Deaths and Marriages: they have to be sealed with some sort of lead seal!'

'The seals were apparently intact before the bodies were interfered with here in the Colony. According to Macarthur, the dissection and the suturing –'

'– and the bloody *glueing*!'

'– were done in China before the coffins were sealed.'

'*Why?*'

'I don't know.' Feiffer, gazing in the direction of the tent and at the figure of John Yin watching it, said softly, 'I don't know, Neal. I have absolutely no idea at all.' He knew what the Commander was going to say next. Feiffer, shaking his head, said, 'The first one, Hwa Cheuk Kuen, died only a week or two ago. The woman, Mrs Ping, has been in the ground here for over a year.'

He was grasping at straws. The Commander asked, 'Where did they die in China and of what?'

'Hwa was in a car accident and Mrs Ping had a coronary.' Feiffer said quickly, 'Hwa's death certificate was issued at a hospital in Canton and Mrs Ping –'

The Commander said hopefully, 'Yes?'

'– died in Honan.'

'That's almost a thousand miles apart!'

'I'm sorry, Neal.' At the tent, the coffin was being carried like a log towards the morgue van. 'What you'll have to do, I'm afraid –'

'I can't get onto Peking. If you're about to tell me that I have to ring Peking and explain all this to them, you can forget it!'

'Neal, it's going to come out.' Feiffer said quietly, 'You know the Chinese attitude to death and sooner or later this is going to come out. You've been in this Colony almost as long

45

as I have and you know that if the locals get wind of the fact that something funny's happening to the bodies of their dead and the Communists are behind it –'

'I can't ring Peking. They'll think it's some sort of bloody last-ditch trick to throw off the negotiations and –' The Commander, ever aware of the politics of his position, said warningly, 'You give these people even half a reason to mount a publicity campaign against the – to their minds – filthy Imperialist pigs who have been running this Colony for their own venal ends for the last hundred years – and they'll go berserk and have troops crossing the borders in ten minutes with the blessing of the UN and half the uncommitted nations of Asia to restore order!'

'And what the hell are the local Chinese going to do when they find out?!'

'They won't find out! We can keep a lid on it until you've –'

'Until I've what?' Feiffer, gripping the radio, shouted down the line, 'Who the hell do you think you're talking to – bloody Edgar Allan Poe? This isn't some sort of mysterious death at a lonely bloody manor on the Sound – someone in China is chopping up bodies and glueing them back together in the wrong order!' He saw John Yin at the morgue van wiping at his eyes with his hand. 'This may not have occurred to you, but the Taoist religion militates against people who have been dismembered getting into Heaven!' Feiffer said angrily, 'Neal, to even come close to getting a result out of this I'd have to have a thousand men checking every bloody grave in Hong Kong going back to – how long?'

'After three years the Chinese dig up their dead and rebury them in bone-urns!'

'Wonderful. So just the fresh three-year-or-less dead – is that it?' Feiffer said maliciously, 'And how many men can I have! You know, locally born, Taoist Chinese Constables who'll look on the whole thing with total professional disinterest and keep it under their hats?' Feiffer said, 'Or do I just do it all myself?'

'Does John Yin of The Society For Neglected Bones know?' The Commander said, 'He's a friend of yours, isn't he?'

Not any more. 'He suspects. He doesn't know, but he

suspects.' The van had driven off and the PWD men were taking down the tent and glancing at John Yin. The men from the PWD were also Chinese, also Taoists, also, when the lease ran out, to become part of China. Feiffer said, 'Neal, something's happening all at once. The woman Ping was in the ground for thirteen months and nobody bothered about her. Hwa was in the coffin repository for less than ten days and someone thought it important enough to get in there, steal his coffin and actually try to sink it in the harbour –'

'Are you telling me there are going to be more?' In his worst fantasies he could not have come up with anything worse and at a worse time. The Commander said hopelessly, 'That there's going to be a complete body's worth – head, chest, legs, arms, the lot? Before this is over?'

'I don't know.' The Commander had made his life in Hong Kong. He was almost at retirement age and, so far, had covered himself, if not in glory, then in solid, dependable achievement. Feiffer said, 'Neal –'

'What's your next step?'

'To see someone at Births, Deaths and Marriages and then, if I can't get any satisfaction from them, Customs to see what checks were made on the coffins at the border.'

'And then?' The Commander said, 'And then?' There was a catch in his voice. He had made his life in the Colony and his reputation. The Commander said softly, 'I'll ring Peking. All right.' He said so softly that Feiffer had to strain to make out the words, *'Like a child from the womb, like a ghost from the tomb,/I arise and unbuild it again.'* He said almost to himself, 'Shelley.' He made a throat-clearing sound to dispel the mood, but it was unsuccessful.

The Commander said quietly, 'You know, he had a wife called Mary. She wrote a book once – a novel – highly successful. It was called *Frankenstein*.' He asked with what sounded like great sadness in his voice, 'Did you know that, Harry?'

Feiffer said softly, 'No.'

'No, not many people do.' His voice sounded as if it was drifting. He was no longer a young man.

The Commander said suddenly, abruptly, 'All right, do

what you can. The moment I can get permission from the powers-that-be, I'll get on the line to Peking.'

Peking was already on the line. In the Detectives' Room, with all the doors and windows locked tight, O'Yee, his throat as dry as dust, picked up the phone and said in a whisper, 'What?'

It was Auden ringing from a public telephone.

O'Yee said in a strangled gasp, 'Yes?'

'Gun.' Auden was speaking in a whisper. That figured, the Ministry Of External Calm was everywhere. What they did externally, was calm people – permanently. Auden said, 'Colt. .357 magnum, six-inch barrel in quick-release holster, twenty five rounds of hollow-point ammo. In my desk drawer. Under confessions and complaints against officers forms. Locked. Key hidden under chair.' Auden said urgently, 'Get it. Need it. Get it.'

O'Yee said, 'Thanks!' O'Yee said, 'Oh, thanks!' O'Yee said, 'Phil, God bless you!'

He was grateful. He almost broke down and wept. O'Yee said happily, 'Oh, thanks, thanks, thanks!'

He needed all the protection he could get.

He hung up.

Everybody was against the man in the wet beard and turban.

At the public telephone outside the Hong Bay Post Office in Great Shanghai Street, Spencer, seeing Auden's face, said helpfully, 'Look, I can do it, Phil –' He went to pick up the new bag of mail from the pavement. 'Look, if you're not up to it, it's no trouble for me to –' Auden put his foot on Spencer's hand. Spencer said, 'Ouch!'

Auden said, 'No.' He couldn't do it instead. Sikhs didn't have fair skin and dimples. Somewhere, Spencer must have had a suitcase of the damned things – all bad. This time he was supposed to be a free-wheeling, brash, boisterous, bronzed, sandaled, camera-toting Australian tourist. His yellow T-shirt read AUSSIE – NO WUCKING FURRIES. (When someone explained it to him he was going to be horrified.) Auden said, 'No, I started it. I'll finish it. I'm on my own on this one. Everyone has deserted me.' He thought he sounded like Gary

Cooper in *High Noon*. 'Take your hand off my mail-bag!' Auden said, 'You'd never make a Sikh. The Sikhs are warriors!'

'I can be a European down on my luck. I could have got a job delivering mail until –'

Auden said, 'If you were a European down on your luck in Hong Kong, you would have been deported.' The Audens of this world, like the Sikhs, reached a point where, like Gary Cooper, they stopped smiling and started to fight. Luckily, below their peaceful, tranquil exterior their interior had spent years practising their fast draws. Auden said, 'I've got my own sunglasses now.' He had a pair of opaque Polaroid shades he had filched from an open parcel in the dead-letter office. Auden said, 'Now no law-breaker is safe.'

'I wouldn't necessarily have been deported. I could have –'

'*I* would have deported you!' Auden said, 'Now, look, you go off and wander around as bloody Olivia Newton-John or Kenny the Koala or whoever you're supposed to be and you keep taking your bloody little photographs, but when someone comes up to me with a bloody great invisible incendiary bomb ready to turn me into a bloody Saigon Buddhist monk, you just keep well out of the way!' He didn't need his gun. He had his innate viciousness. Auden, shouldering the bag and taking no notice of Spencer examining his bruised hand, said, 'OK? Is that clear?'

'Phil, I'm not sure that someone is actually putting incendiary bombs into the sacks.' His sandals hurt. Spencer taking the left one off and standing there in character like some sort of hippy about to chew on his footwear said thoughtfully, 'I'm not too sure that it isn't something in the mail-sack like the letters or –'

'We've checked the letters!' Give Spencer a pipe and a pound of cocaine and he would have set up shop in Baker Street. Auden said, 'We've looked at them, we've picked them up and scrunched them, we've even X-rayed them – there's nothing in the letters but letters!' He was ready. He turned to go.

He was still chewing on the sandal. His eyes had that far away look. It was time to leave. Spencer, shaking his head, said, 'Funny about the wrong address on that Hawaiian postcard – the dead-letter man checked everything with us before we left. Funny he wouldn't have known there was no such address.'

He didn't care. He was ready. Auden said, 'Hmm.' Auden said, 'It was a postcard of Waikiki Beach with real sand stuck on it.' Auden, staring out at the empty streets at high noon, said, 'Who cares?'

'The dead-letter man did. He put it ever so carefully into his pocket.'

The head prefect. *Ever* so carefully. Auden said irritably, 'I'm ready to go. I'm psyched up. *Can we go?*'

Neither rain nor sleet nor snow . . .

Out there, in the streets, somewhere in the struggling mass of humanity, there was someone with a little invisible incendiary bomb waiting to blow him up. Auden said softly, 'Hmmph!' He said softly, 'Hm, hm, hm.'

Yup.

Behind his opaque sunglasses, like Gary Cooper in *High Noon*, he narrowed his eyes in anticipation.

He was alone.

He was unarmed.

He was ready.

Yup.

He was looking forward to it.

In the closed-in courtyard at the back of the Government Mortuary, Mr Kan of Kan's Western Heaven Coffin Repository, leaning in the window of Mrs Hwa's car, said softly, 'No, they won't release him to me.' He still wore his embroidered robe and skull cap of office, the symbol of the generations. 'I'm sorry.' The fingernail of the little finger on his left hand was long and carefully manicured: a symbol that he was of the scholar class and did no manual work. Mr Kan, touching at it with his other hand and twisting at it, said softly in Cantonese, 'The fates are against you. You are in the hands of foreigners and there is no appeal.' He said again with a shrug, 'I am truly sorry.'

She was not used to riding in cars. She had begun life as a peasant – a field hand – and even when her husband had bought her a car and paid for her to learn how to drive it she had hardly ever done more with it than wash it for him. Mrs Hwa said softly, 'Did they allow you to use their telephone?'

'Oh, yes. Of course.' Mr Kan wore a round jade Pi, the symbol of heaven and the unity of opposites, around his neck. He touched at it with his long fingernail. 'Yes, of course.'

'You rang Mr John Yin of The Society For Neglected Bones?'

'He said your husband had you, still alive, and that his grave and soul were, therefore, being well looked after.' Mr Kan said awkwardly, 'The message was relayed to me by someone in his office. Mr Yin is out. He will not talk to me directly.' There was no need to apologize. Mrs Hwa was also a Taoist and devout. She knew that there should be no doors to the place where coffins were housed, only talismans. Mr Kan said softly, 'I do not know what is happening.' He looked back to the closed rear door to the mortuary and wondered what, behind its locks, it hid.

Mr Kan said with quiet acceptance in Mandarin, the scholar language of China, '*Ta chia tu shih ming, pan tien pu yu jên.*' He seemed a little lost, and sad. He said in Cantonese, translating the proverb for her so she would understand its meaning, 'Our destinies have been set with no reference to our wishes at all.'

He said softly to the weeping woman, 'I am sorry.'

It was her again. It was the Ministry Of External Calm.

O'Yee, ready for her, having practised and rehearsed, girded his loins, strengthened his self-image, motivated his motivations, said firmly, as he had promised he would say when the time came – '*Ack –*'

'Christopher?'

It was a local call. She sounded close.

On the phone, O'Yee said, 'Ack – ah – frrmph –' It was a sort of drowning noise.

She was quoting. She was quoting from Thoreau. She was getting it right. She had money. The Ministry had a *budget*. Miss Fan said in her soft Southern voice, 'Our life is frittered away by detail . . . Simplify, *simplify* . . . !'

O'Yee said, 'Ummph . . . ?'

She made a soft ironic chuckling sound, one philosopher to another. '"As if you could kill time without injuring all of eternity . . ."'

He had read that one. It was in *Walden*. In his edition *injuring* had been spelled 'inhuring'. She didn't have a pirate edition, she had the real thing. She had a budget. O'Yee said, 'Humm – ah . . .' He wanted to go to the toilet. He wanted to put his glasses on, but his hands were shaking. O'Yee said 'Umm . . .'

'"Some circumstantial evidence is very strong, as when you find a trout in the milk."' Her voice was neutral. There was a pause. (It could have gone on forever. O'Yee's brain had stopped functioning.) Miss Fan said pointedly, '"Our life is frittered away by detail . . . simplify, *simplify*!"'

She said urgently in Cantonese, 'Detective Senior Inspector O'Yee, find me. Now. *Find me!*'

In Wyang Street, the Resurrection Squad had stopped their Mercedes car to check their destination on a map. They had been travelling the wrong way, north towards Yellowthread Street and The Peak, when the place they wanted was on the waterfront near the resettlement area and the slums off Wyang Road. They needed to make a left down Cat Street and then another left into Beach Road and then down towards Fisherman's Beach off Hop Pei Cove.

There were six of them in the big, powerful vehicle, all young healthy Southern Chinese with close-cropped hair and ramrod-stiff bearing.

In the rear seat, the man with the map leaned forward and gave directions to the driver in rapid Mandarin and, to make sure the driver understood, pointed with his finger through the traffic towards Cat Street where the turn had to be made.

The man with the map said as he folded it and put it carefully into a khaki-covered map case at his feet where the entrenching tools and shovels were arranged, 'All right? Understood?' He glanced at his watch. They had time to spare.

'Yes, sir.' The driver, starting the engine, flicked the indicator lever on his steering wheel to signal his intention to go out and join the traffic. He wanted no trouble from the police. In careful, military fashion, he waited for a break in the traffic and then, the indicator light at the rear of the car flashing, with due care and attention, at regulation, lawful speed, made the turn into Cat Street towards the south.

None of the six men smoked, and, in the car, with the air-conditioning at its lowest level, there was only the smell about them of healthy, light perspiration and, from the shovels and the entrenching tools at their feet, the fading lingering odour of exhumation and death.

5

'Births, Deaths and Marriages on the island said I'd find you here.' At the open glass door of the office on the top floor of the Kowloon railways goods marshalling yards administration building, Feiffer, showing his warrant card, said to the shirt-sleeved European standing at the open window gazing down at the confusion of trains, tracks, trucks and tumult, 'Detective Chief Inspector Feiffer of Yellowthread Street.' The tracks of the marshalling yards led across the twenty or so miles of open country across the New Territories to China. By the volume of it, so did the noise. There was a long goods train passing directly under the window. Its noise came in and filled the document-strewn, pigeon-holed room like a jackhammer. The man had not heard him. Feiffer, taking a step into the room, his ears ringing, shouted, 'Mr Owens?'

'I heard you the first time.' Turning, he was a short, rotund, red-faced man in his early fifties with watery blue eyes. 'There's nothing wrong with my hearing. Births, Deaths and Marriages rang me after you saw them.' The train below was passing, going north. Thank God, so was its noise. Owens, gazing after it wistfully for a moment, said briskly, 'You were lucky to catch me. I'm taking the 6.10 to Canton this evening and I won't be back until tomorrow night.' If he worked for Births, Deaths and Marriages it looked as if he had strayed into the wrong office. The little room was full of pictures of trains. Owens said in a melodic Welsh valleys accent (before that it

54

had been a matter of reading his lips), 'Owens, Special Consignments.' He saw Feiffer glance at a collection of train
nameplates on the wall and the cryptic semi-circular metal
sign filched or souvenired from a cutting somewhere:
т 3 ½ WHISTLE. Owens said, 'I handle the legal and administrative liaison between BD and M and the railways concerning
the movement of dead bodies on trains.' There was an ageing
Union Pacific nameplate above a framed photograph of
Owens at a golden spike commemorative ceremony somewhere in America. In the photograph he was wearing a striped
American engine driver's cap. Owens, reading the legend on
the plate, said proudly, '*The Matthew Brady*' – he was a
famous photographer during the American Civil War – that's
a rare one, that is.'

So was he. Feiffer, putting his warrant card back into his
pocket, said evenly, 'Are you the person who views and
certifies the bodies of people who die in China for their entry
into Hong Kong?'

'I am. Yes.' He had a fob watch on a silver chain in his pants
pocket. He took it out and looked at it. Owens said, 'British
Rail. They sold off all the drivers' pocket watches a few years
ago and gave them digital Jap crap instead.'

There was another train coming. The noise was terrible.
Feiffer, grimacing at it and raising his voice, shouted, 'Why do
you have an office here if you work for Births, Deaths and
Marriages?'

'I wangled it!' He was a one hundred per cent, dyed-in-the-
soot train nut. Owens said with monumental superfluity, 'I like
trains.'

At least the trains were diesels. Coal burners passing directly
below the open window fifty or a hundred times a day was a
thought too appalling to contemplate.

Owens said, 'They rang me to give me time to dig out the
files.' He nodded in the direction of his desk where a model of
Stephenson's Rocket held down a pile of documents and files.
'You're interested in one Hwa Cheuk Kuen, male deceased,
special consignment from China, and one Ping Kit-Ling,
female deceased, also special consignment from China.' The
train below the window was stopped and idling. Owens,

55

gazing down at it, said easily, 'They both died while on visits to the People's Republic of China, both were perfectly ordinary cases of natural or accidental causes, both were viewed and certified by this office, and both were carried back as special consignments and handed over to the appropriate, documented undertaker or mortician.' It was all in the files. He seemed to be watching the train in case it did something really interesting like grow wings. Owens asked with a trace of irritation in his voice, 'What else do you want to know?'

'I want to know what happened to them between the time you or a member of your staff – (Owens said, 'Me. I don't have any staff.') – between the time you saw them in their coffins in China and the time they were handed over to the appropriate undertaker here in Hong Kong.' He was the sort of man who didn't care whether the trains ran on time or not, just so long as there were trains. 'I want to know the procedure.'

'Standard procedure.' He seemed to think he was stating the obvious. Owens said, 'As coffins are all over the world on trains, they were listed on the manifest as urgent medical supplies.'

'Were the coffins sealed?'

'Of course.'

'By you?'

'Do you mean sealed or closed?'

'I mean both.'

'Yes. Of course they were.'

'Where?'

The train below was still idling. Owens said offhandedly, 'In Canton.'

'That was Mr Hwa. And for Mrs Ping?'

'What do you mean?'

'She died in Honan province.' It was an effort not to take the man and shake him. Feiffer said with an effort at calmness that was far from successful, 'Mr Hwa died in Canton in a car accident. Mrs Ping, according to the Death Certificate which you no doubt sighted and which you no doubt have a copy of, died from cardiac arrest in Honan province.'

'It doesn't matter where she died. All the viewing and

certification is done in Canton.' He sensed the anger. He closed the window.

'Why in Canton?'

'Because that's where it's done.' It was all in the files. Owens, going to them and tapping them, said easily, 'All the bodies of Hong Kong Chinese – in fact all the bodies that require exiting from China for reburial or disposal elsewhere – are sent to a central point in Canton – to the Canton Military Hospital – and there examined, certified and documented and sealed for onward destinations.' He said before Feiffer could, 'It's on the train line, you see. An old military spur. The role of the Special Consignments man – me – is to travel up to Canton and, having satisfied myself that the body is who the Chinese say it is, collect the death certificate, arrange the manifest and seal the coffin with Births, Deaths and Marriages government seals against tampering so it can clear Customs at the frontier without being opened.' He saw Feiffer glance at a tiny safe in the corner of the room. 'No, that's an antique mail-safe from the old Great Western Line in England. The seals are held by Births, Deaths and Marriages in their vault and changed every week for security. I've got a job in Canton tonight with a Hong Kong contract worker who died of a stroke on a building site near Shanghai. Even I won't know what the current official seal will look like until it's delivered to me at the station ten minutes before the train goes.' He asked, 'Why? Has someone been accused of smuggling heroin in coffins?'

'Not exactly, no.'

'Good. Because it can't be done.'

'They're lead seals?'

'They are. And they're impressed with an official bronze seal press that would take something approaching the facilities of the Royal Mint to forge.' Owens said, 'In fact the Royal Mint makes them.' He was unworried, sure of his procedures. Somewhere, by the look on his face, he had an ace. Owens said, 'Anything else?'

In the files Feiffer could see sheets of what looked like letterheaded documents. He knew what the letterhead was and why Owens looked smug.

Feiffer said, 'And then the seals are checked again by –?'

Owens said, 'By Customs. They're all stopped at the border, taken off the train and the seals checked before they come in here to me.'

It was hot in the room. He didn't even sweat. 'And then I check the seals again here at the Freight Office. And then before the coffins are handed over, the seals are checked again.' He smiled. That ended the problem.

Outside the train was starting up again. It didn't end the problem. It was the problem. Owens, going to the window to look out, said firmly, conclusively, 'All right?'

'Before the Chinese normally exhume the bodies of their relatives for re-interment in a bone-urn and reburial on private land they usually leave the original coffin in the ground for three years.' Feiffer asked, afraid of the answer, 'In the last three years approximately, how many bodies have come in from China as special consignments through your office?'

'Three hundred and thirty-seven – and the two who'll come in tomorrow or the next day: the two fishermen – three hundred and thirty-nine.' Owens said, nodding, 'I've got all the files in my cabinets, each one of them, all of them.' He was a man who liked trains. Nothing was ever going to be allowed to hurt them. Owens, pausing, listening as the train began gathering speed, lapping it up, drinking in the sound like a lover, said helpfully, 'If you like I can have all of them photostatted and sent over to your office . . .'

All over the world, governments were ripping up the train tracks because they were costly and inefficient and replacing them with bus lanes. It was not going to happen in Hong Kong.

He asked, 'All right? Shall I do that?' He said easily, 'No trouble at all.' He almost said, 'Next time, take the train.' He heard the sound outside. He was happy. It wasn't until after his wife and children had left him that he had discovered how much there really was in the world of the railways.

He listened to the sound of the diesel and wished only that it could have been steam.

He said helpfully, smiling, 'Always happy to assist.' He didn't give a damn. He went to his window and looked out.

*

Ringing the Bank of China – which everyone knew was the headquarters of all the subversion the Colony had suffered in the last thirty years – was, as always, an exercise in self-abasement.

On the phone O'Yee, perspiring profusely, said in a small voice, 'Miss Fan, please?'

They always hung up on you. The man's voice at the other end of the line said in Cantonese, 'What?' He was going to hang up.

O'Yee said, '"I frequently tramped eight or ten miles through the deepest snow to keep an appointment with a beech-tree, or a yellow birch, or an old acquaintance among the pines . . ."'

The voice at the other end of the line said in Cantonese, 'What?' He was going to hang up.

O'Yee said trembling, 'Ministry of External Calm, please.'

The voice at the other end of the line said with sudden interest, 'Who is this?'

O'Yee said, '*What!?*'

He hung up.

In the radio in his beard Spencer's voice said helpfully, 'Maybe it was the stamp.' Now he was a bloody postcard expert. 'Actually, Phil, some of the early Hawaiian stamps are very valuable.'

The postcard with the Waikiki sand on it the dead-letter man had taken had had a standard US postage stamp. So did the two other identical postcards he had in his bag to deliver this time. They both showed people looking important no one had ever heard of. Auden said, 'Hmm.' He peered up and down Jade Street for men with bombs.

'The 1851 two-cents blue, for example, or the five-cents blue or the thirteen-cents blue.' Spencer asked, 'Was the stamp blue?' He thought about it. Thirteen cents in 1851 wouldn't buy a hell of a lot. Spencer asked, 'Did the postcard go by sea or by air?'

It had gone by detonation. Auden said into his beard, 'Shut up.' He was thinking. Auden said, 'Where are you?' How could you hide in a yellow T-shirt? Auden said, 'I can't see you anywhere.'

'I'm across the street in a fruit market by the bananas.'

Auden said, 'Good.' He had finally found his niche. Auden said, 'Stay there.' He hefted his mail-bag. All up and down the street there were suspicious-looking people with things in their hands. It was hot. It was almost high noon. In *High Noon* everybody hated the man with the tin star. Everybody was out to get him. All his friends had deserted him. Lucky bastard. Auden said, not into his radio, but into his beard, 'This is up to me.' In *The Fastest Gun Alive*, Glenn Ford had been a harmless-looking dope too. Little did anyone know. Auden, flexing his giant fist and crushing two letters into pulp, said in a firm, calm tone, 'You leave this to me.' There were some things a man had to do alone. Auden said, 'OK?' He looked for the man who in State Prison swore it would be my life or his'n.

Spencer's voice said with sudden interest, 'If you put a combination of all the rare Hawaiian stamps on a postcard you'd get enough for airmail postage.' It had been a movie. The letter with the McGuffin on it – the stamps – had been in the hero's pocket all along. The postcard was in the dead-letter man's pocket. Spencer said, 'But wait a minute. In the movie the letter was never posted.' He asked, 'If the US Post Office put a postmark on a line of valuable stamps – a modern postmark – surely that'd destroy their value.' He asked, 'Don't you think so, Phil?' He had strayed from the banana counter to the capsicums. He was conspicuous. Spencer, stepping back into the yellow, said suddenly, 'The Hawaiian stamps are under the modern stamps!' It didn't work. Spencer said, 'But then, why would the dead-letter man blow up his valuable stamps if he was sending them to the wrong address? All he'd have to do was look at the postcard when it came in, take the valuable stamps and send the undeliverable postcards back to Hawaii.' Spencer said, 'It's not against the law to send rare stamps through the mail anyway.' He asked, 'Did you see if the postcard had a return address on it?'

Auden said, 'Spencer –' He went into a hallway and delivered the mail. The boxes were all, of course, set in the darkest part of the place. The people who lived in the place were obviously scum. They hadn't even taken in the mail he had delivered on his first run. Auden, scrunching himself down from the shoulders, readying himself to do a little bomb catching, said in a burst of static, 'Shut up.' He was ready. God, he was ready. All he needed was Grace Kelly dressed up in her Quaker gear and breakfast oats smile and he was right. Auden, his eyes flickering back and forth in the dark corridor, aware of every minuscule movement of the dust, cockroaches and creaking, said in a whisper, 'Let a man do the work he's fitted for.' He wasn't the man who shot Liberty Valance, he was the man who shot Liberty Valance while the man who thought he had shot Liberty Valance was about to be shot by Liberty Valance. And the man who really shot Liberty Valance was . . . He had to be useful for something. Auden, snarling, said into his radio, 'You go to the movies – who was the man who really shot Liberty Valance?'

It was the Polynesian. He was sneaky enough to have crept up behind anyone and shot them. The Polynesian, appearing out of nowhere, towering over him, demanded, 'Where's my mail?'

'John Wayne, I think. Didn't he shoot him in the back?' Spencer said irritably, 'Look, about these stamps . . .'

'I haven't had any mail for days!' He was a Polynesian. You could almost see his sharpened teeth. The Polynesian, reaching down and hauling the scrunched-up Gary Cooper to his feet, said menacingly, 'It's no use cowering there –'

(Auden tried to say, 'I'm not cowering!' but nothing came out. It didn't when you cowered.)

'– I wait for you in the street and there's no mail, I wait in my apartment watching you deliver through my keyhole and there's no mail, and now, I catch you sneaking around in the hallway peering into mail-boxes and talking to yourself and there's no mail!' The Polynesian said, 'I thought the Hong Kong Post Office was supposed to be efficient.' They had Indians in Polynesia too. The Polynesian demanded, 'What sort of Sikh are you to be talking to yourself like an old woman at a lu-au.' He heard the door behind him open. It was a Melanesian (same ocean, different islands, frizzy hair). The Polynesian, still holding Auden by the scruff of the neck demanded, 'You! Brother! Don't tell me you're waiting for mail too?'

If he had had his .357 magnum you would have seen a few grass skirts fly. Auden, choking, said desperately into his beard radio, 'Ack, ugg, ack!' As usual Spencer took no notice.

'I've had nothing for a week!' The Melanesian was some sort of New Guinean. Auden was some sort of Indian. For some sort of reason, the New Guinean said in pidgin as to an idiot boy, 'Hey, letters bilong this fella here – you got?'

For a moment Auden saw into his open room. It was full of cased butterflies.

After they had beaten him to a pulp – he saw the Polynesian's teeth – and eaten him, or pinned his wings to the wall – he saw the Melanesian's butterflies – the first thing he was going to do when he got his magnum back from O'Yee was kill him with it. Auden said, 'Ack, ack!' And then Spencer. Auden said, 'Arraagah!' He was being throttled. He heard Spencer's voice at the lowest volume possible, his thinking volume, say on the radio, 'Maybe it's not the postcard . . .' He sounded as if he was eating a banana. Auden writhing, wrenching, said, 'Eeerrkkk!' Auden said in a gasp of air the Polynesian let him have on strictly humanitarian grounds, or, more likely, by accident, 'I'm not a mailman at all!'

The Melanesian put his hand onto his door to slam it in his face. The Melanesian said with disgust, 'That's for sure!' He said something to his fellow Pacific-dweller in a language that could have been anything from Sandwich Island to Samoan. Whatever it was, translated into Punjabi it would have restarted the Khyber Pass massacre. The Melanesian said, shaking his head, 'The man's an idiot. He talks to himself.'

On the beard radio Spencer said with a banana in his mouth, 'I don't know . . . What do you think, Phil?'

The Melanesian said, 'Pugh!'

He slammed his door.

The Polynesian said, 'Pah!'

He let Auden go and stalked away down the hallway out into the street.

The idiot said, 'Oohh . . .'

He slid down the wall against the mail-boxes holding his neck.

Spencer said happily, 'Phil? Are you thinking about it?'

The mailbag, against the wall, went 'Psst!'

Spencer said, 'What was that?'

Auden said, 'Oh, shit . . .!' He looked. On the wall of the hallway, in a glass case, there was a large fire bucket full of water. Auden, not the man who shot Liberty Valance or even the man who thought he had shot Liberty Valance while the man who really shot Liberty Valance shot Liberty Valance was shooting him, but poor old, misunderstood Liberty himself, said sadly, 'Oh . . . no . . .'

In the hallway, happy, joyfully, with a complete, full life of its own, his bag blew up.

Three o'clock in the afternoon. CLOSED FOR REDEVELOP-MENT AND LAND RECLAMATION.

At the deserted paupers' graveyard off the shanty town near Hop Pei Cove, the Resurrection Squad, standing a little way from their car, glanced over the lie of the land and back to the traffic on Beach Road.

The traffic was still heavy, full of commercial vehicles and fruit trucks and delivery men.

The cemetery was due to be turned into a parking lot in six months time when the last of the dead buried in it had passed their requisite three years in the ground and could be disinterred and placed in bone-urns on a hill somewhere in the New Territories. It was the Chinese way: the time was fixed by the dates of the deaths to the instant.

There was no structure in the little half-acre section of fenced-off land, no hut nor cemetery keeper to watch over it. The gods, and the spirits, and the past lives of the dead, were sufficient.

The six young men in the Squad were lean and fit and even in the heat they did not perspire. They were unafraid. There was nothing personal involved in it.

3 p.m.

It was still too early.

They were not from Hong Kong, but they were Chinese and

they knew that wherever there were Chinese there were Chinese restaurants.

3 p.m.

Without discussion, they went back to their car to consult their map to find somewhere to have a light, filling meal.

'Tomorrow's another day, Phil . . .'

The last time at the cemetery where they had got the Ping woman had been too risky, but they had had to be sure that what was supposed to be there had been there. It had. In the back of the car, the man with the map, rubbing at his chin, closed his eyes in thought. *Kwang Ting Nam*: he had the corpse's name written in careful block characters on a sheet of paper in his pocket.

Kwan Ting Nam. He had seen the little grave marker. It was in the exact centre of the graveyard, on a slight hillock, well in sight of the traffic on Beach Road.

'Sir?' The driver was waiting for an order. 'Captain?' He heard someone tap against their seat impatiently.

3.04 p.m. Too early. Too early.

The Captain said suddenly, 'We'll eat.' He glanced back over his shoulder through the window at the graveyard. It was there, waiting for them. It would still be there tonight. The Captain, as if it irked him that he had hesitated, ordered them all, 'Go. I said we'll stop to eat, so do it.'

He ordered the driver in Mandarin, 'And you, this isn't a tank, it's an expensive German motor car, so drive it like one.' He said to no one in particular, mainly to himself, 'We've waited for this for almost two thousand years so a few more hours isn't going to make any difference at all.'

He saw they were all struck by the thought.

He ordered the driver briskly, 'Take the first left, then a right, then a right again.'

He ordered the man sharply, 'Go!'

'Bank of China . . .'

'Oh . . .'

The other phone rang and he hung up.

The other phone was Miss Fan. Miss Fan said as if he had forgotten to do it, 'Find me! Locate me! *Find me!*'

'Oh . . . !'

He hung up.

Gary Cooper in *High Noon* would have said, '. . . Yup . . .' Gary Cooper wasn't lying on his back on the step of a stinking hallway in Jade Street dripping fire-bucket water.

Gary Cooper would have pressed on and only looked a little more determined and haggard.

Gary Cooper didn't have Sikh make-up dripping down his face and a still smouldering shirt on his back.

Gary Cooper didn't have Detective Inspector Bill Spencer standing over him in a yellow T-shirt. Gary Cooper had had Grace Kelly.

It wasn't high noon. It was 3.15 p.m.

Gary Cooper would have stayed.

Auden said, 'I'm going home.'

Gary Cooper would have said . . .

Who the hell cared what Gary Cooper would have said!

Auden said, 'Spencer –!'

Spencer said with real concern, 'Yes, Phil? What? Anything.'

Auden said, 'Spencer!'

'Yes?'

Oh, Pancho . . . Oh, Cisco . . .

Auden said sadly, destroyed at every single turn, 'Oh . . . *SPENCER!*'

6

2.06 *a.m.* 'Macarthur says it's a butcher.'

He got no response. There was none to make. The Commander was dressed in a dinner jacket under his lightweight topcoat. He smelled slightly of brandy. He had been at a dinner party when his office had called him. He had a small rolled-gold Dunhill lighter in his hand and, no doubt, in a leather case in his inside pocket, equally expensive cigars. The Commander, turning the lighter over and over in his hand, asked, 'Who reported it, Harry?' It was not the time for cigars. He put the lighter back into his coat pocket.

'A squad car from North Point. They were in pursuit of a stolen car and they noticed the lights. By the time they caught the car and called in the message it was all over.' He nodded to where PCs Sun and Lee were erecting a black plastic screen around the open grave. They had done only a makeshift job and, in the lights of the cars parked off from the hillock and the reflection of the moon in the harbour, you could still see the end of the coffin protruding from the hole. 'They were about to rebury it when the siren must have frightened them off.' Behind the half-acre paupers' cemetery across Beach Road there were the corrugated-iron and packing-case shanties of the poor. Feiffer could smell the kerosene from their lanterns. He needed a cigarette, but it was not the time or the place. Feiffer, glancing back at the shanties and the lights and the crowds starting to form along the street, said quietly, 'The lid of the coffin has been crowbarred open and then nailed roughly shut again.'

'You haven't opened it or tried to see inside?'

'No. I've got a call into the GMO Doctor Macarthur, and John Yin of The Society For Neglected Bones is coming.' The smell from the open grave was dissipating with the kerosene fumes and the activity. Before, when he had first arrived, it had been terrible. Feiffer said definitely, 'No, it hasn't been touched.'

'What about your PCs?'

'No.' They were Chinese. They would have walked across burning coals to avoid touching it. The screen was proceeding slowly. It was a screen made of split-open plastic trash bags, held up by bamboo poles. At half past one in the morning, without Macarthur and his exhumation tent, there had been nothing else. On the harbour there were only the running lights of a few fishing junks coming back to port or going out to sea and, in the middle of Summer, in the absence of wind, there was a coldness to it. Feiffer said hopefully, 'All we expect to find in the coffin is bones.' The date of death on the headstone had been almost two and a half years ago. He needed the cigarette. He took one from his pocket and lit it. Feiffer said, 'Unless you've had a good response from Peking I'm going to have to tell John Yin what's going on.' It was a statement. At the open grave the Chinese constables looked nervous. They kept putting their hands in their tunic pockets to touch at talismans they kept there. Feiffer said firmly, 'He has to know.' He knew where the Commander had been with his brandy and cigars. Feiffer said quietly, 'They won't let you ring, will they? The Government?'

'They say it's politically inexpedient to have dealings with China at this time on a matter of this nature.' The Commander, holding out his hand for one of Feiffer's cigarettes and lighting it from Feiffer's box of matches, said, looking away towards the shanties and the crowds gathering at the cemetery fence in the street, 'They take the line that it's probably a murder cover-up, that some depraved member of the criminal classes' – he said with a bleak smile, 'Yes, people do still talk that way – that some small-time thug murdered one of his partners in crime and used the coffins to dispose of the body a piece at a time.' He raised his hand. 'I didn't point out that if he was taking parts of bodies already in the ground to hide parts of bodies he wanted to dispose of that he'd still be left with one complete body. They think it's a storm in a teacup, one of the little inexplicable footnotes to their memoirs of fifty years in the exotic East.' The Commander said, 'Unless this gets worse –'

It was getting worse. Feiffer said, 'Then I intend to tell John Yin everything that's happened.'

'All right.' The cigarette in the Commander's hand was burning away. In the reflected light from the cars and the harbour he looked old and tired. At the grave the plastic screen was up, Lee and Sun standing guard around it. It was 2.10 a.m., still and windless.

'It isn't finished, Neal. Whatever's going on here has only just started.' At the grave the two Chinese constables were afraid of ghosts. They were afraid of whatever was there inside the darkness of the rotting coffin. He could smell the smell of death and eternity when he had first arrived and the coffin had still been moving in the open grave as the earth around it subsided and slipped. Feiffer said with difficulty, 'I think what we're going to find in that coffin –'

'My God, Harry, you were born in Hong Kong. Your father was born here! He was a cop in Shanghai for God knows how long and you've been a cop here for –' The Commander, trying to find something to do with the cigarette in his hand, said desperately, 'How many bloody Chinese dialects do you speak? Three? Four? And bloody Mandarin and Cantonese better than half the native speakers – you must have heard of something like this happening before!' It was hopeless. They all knew what they were going to find in the coffin. All around him he could smell the smell of the kerosene lamps of the shanty dwellers. He could smell the smell of China. 'Death is the biggest thing in the Chinese calendar – they're like the bloody Irish – half of them buy their coffins with the first pay packet they earn at age fourteen. There are stories of how in order to make sure a dead noble faced the right way on his funeral train in 1901 – not millennia ago – but in *1901* the

Chinese railways moved an entire train line around a mountain! You can't have lived here so long and not have any idea at all what's going on here now!' The Commander said angrily, 'Where the hell's Macarthur?'

'He's still at the morgue. He was doing a second PM on the Ping woman –'

'We can't wait.' The Commander, shaking his head, said firmly, 'We can't wait. If we wait –' He saw a flash of light from the street as someone opened a car door and then, after a word with one of the other Chinese constables there, came quickly across towards the grave. The Commander, going towards him, called, 'Mr Yin! John Yin!' The cigarette in his hand had gone out. He put it quickly in his mouth and relit it with his gold lighter. Turning, he called back to Feiffer, 'Right! We won't wait.' At the open grave, behind the screens, there were crowbars and shovels brought from Yellowthread Street by the two Chinese constables. He caught Yin half way up and, taking him by the hand in a handshake that held him briefly where he was, speaking Cantonese so everyone would know exactly what was coming, the Commander ordered, 'Detective Chief Inspector Feiffer, we'll have that coffin completely out of the ground, please, so we can see just what we've got here tonight.'

He still had Yin's hand held in his grip. The Commander putting his other hand gently on Yin's shoulder, making sure the cigarette did not burn the cloth of his expensive suit, said reassuringly, 'Mr Yin, if you would, you stay by me as a witness –'

2.38 a.m. 'Kwang Ting Nam, age 57 years, pauper.' John Yin, reading from a scrap of paper in his hand in the light of a gas lamp hung on one of the bamboo poles near the open coffin, said in Cantonese with no expression in his voice, 'Truck driver's mate. He was accidentally killed inside the Chinese border at Sham Chun when struck by falling crates.' The scrap of paper was a photostatic copy of the death certificate extracted from the Society's files. 'His bones were due to be taken from the cemetery here in six months to be re-interred in the New Territories where he lived.' He looked into the rotting open coffin at the bones and the disintegrating scraps of linen around them. 'He was brought back on the train from the Canton military hospital where he was pronounced dead.' There was a silence. Yin said softly in Cantonese, 'They're not all here, are they? His bones?'

'No.' The bones had slipped to the bottom of the coffin the first time it had been hauled out of the ground. They made a pathetic collection of nothing more than yellowed ivory in the ripped open coffin, things of no importance that a dog would have dug up. Feiffer said quietly, 'The pelvis and both legs and feet are missing.' He asked Yin with sudden hope, 'The accident. When he –?'

'He was intact.' The spine was twisted and fractured, black where in life it had been torn open and the marrow exposed. Yin said quietly, 'No.' His mouth was trembling. He could not control it. All around him he could smell the smell of the kerosene lamps of the poor. Yin said, unable to control the smell of the trembling of his mouth, 'No. He was intact. *He was a person!*'

2.51 *a.m.* 'The Canton military hospital, Neal . . . !'

'No, no one. No one at all in China.' The Commander, shaking his head, said, 'I can't ring anyone at all.'

'Look at these damned seals again! The coffin supposedly came into the Colony unopened. Supposedly, according to Owens, it was –'

The seals around the coffin were corroded, black lead. The Commander, still shaking his head, refusing to look at the seal in Feiffer's hand, said, 'No. It was done here. What-ever happened after the coffin was sealed and imported into the Colony was done here. The seals are genuine. The seals on the other two coffins were genuine. I had them checked.'

'It wasn't done here! It was done in China! In China the body was hacked up and sewn up and then bloody glued with parts of another body and *then* it was sealed!'

'No. Owens viewed the bodies intact before they were put on the train.'

'Is that the politically expedient line?'

70

'That's the truthful, one hundred per cent genuine line! Owens is trustworthy. I checked. He's trusted.'

'By whom?'

'By the Hong Kong government, by Births, Deaths and Marriages and, more importantly –'

'By the Chinese whom you're not allowed to contact –' Feiffer, trying not to look at Yin's face or the thing the grave robbers had left in the coffin, said with sudden anger, 'He's some sort of lunatic who spends his time staring out of windows into the chimney stacks of bloody trains sniffing up diesel fumes the way other people sniff cocaine! Who trusts him – the bloody International Guild of Demented Train-Spotters?' The lead seal in his hand had a white oxide eating it away. The powder came off in his hand. 'Looking at the bloody pictures on his wall and some of the souvenirs he's picked up, he must spend half his bloody life riding around on trains all over the world!'

'He can afford it. He isn't some sort of underpaid cop, he's an upper-grade civil servant.' He had had his orders. The Commander, shaking his head, said with no further room for argument, 'If Owens says he sealed the coffins in Canton and then rechecked the seals here in Hong Kong before he handed them out then whatever was done to the coffins was done here in Hong Kong and the Chinese government and/or the Canton military hospital isn't involved!' He dropped his voice. 'Harry, have you any idea what an enquiry to the military in Canton would open up?' He had had the notion explained to him in no uncertain terms at his dinner party over the cigars and brandy. The Commander said in echo of the explanation, 'Why the hell don't we just declare war on the bloody Communist Chinese and have done with it?'

He heard a voice speaking in low Cantonese. It was John Yin. Yin said again, in English, so he would understand it perfectly, 'Not even the Communists would do something like this.'

'If the seals haven't been faked then Owens has to have been in on it!'

'There has to be another explanation.'

'*What?*'

71

'I don't know. That's your job. You're the bloody detective!' The Commander said, 'Detect. Earn your bloody money!'

'Soon, in a few years, the Communists will have control of Hong Kong the way they have control of Macao now.' It was Yin's voice. He was speaking not to any of them, but to the two Chinese constables. He was speaking in English. He thought they did not understand it. Yin said quietly, 'And then a few years after that Hong Kong will become a special administrative region of the People's Republic and they will have complete control.' He looked down into the open coffin and then away towards the lights of the harbour. Yin said, 'The Communists would not have done this. Not now. They would not have done it.' Across from China there was still the island of Taiwan, still, forty years on, run by their enemies the Nationalists. The war between them had never officially ended, but now it was no longer fought with guns but with victories in the media. Yin said, 'No. It is stupid, pointless.' He looked down into the coffin with the eyes of a man from the oldest civilization on Earth. 'It is not the way a Chinese of any worth would think.' He said suddenly in Cantonese, clenching his fist to catch something in the air that was not there, 'Why? *Why is this happening?*'

3.18 a.m. 'It's a butcher's amputation straight through the spine, done without skill.' With the flesh all gone in post mortem adipose decomposition there were no sutures or glue, but like the others, they had been there. Doctor Macarthur, slipping off his rubber gloves and getting up from his knees at the side of the coffin, said, not by way of explanation or apology, but as a preamble to something of interest, 'I was delayed doing a second complete gross and pathological autopsy on the Ping woman, what there was left of her.' His fingers were yellow with nicotine stains from the pungent Gauloise cigarettes he chain-smoked. He lit one now. He looked down into the bones in the open coffin. 'There's nothing much I can tell you about this one.' He asked, 'Was he a porter or a man who carried bags of rice or something?'

Feiffer said curiously, 'He was a truck driver's mate. He loaded and unloaded trucks.'

'Hmm.' Macarthur, grinning at the Commander, said, tapping himself on the chest, 'Sherlock Holmes.' He nodded back down into the coffin. 'Pronounced curvature of the bones of the left shoulder consistent with repeated application of heavy weights.' He glanced at John Yin and wondered who he was. Macarthur said, 'The Ping woman's Death Certificate stated that the suspected cause of death was a heart attack. Since the chest was missing there's no way that can be verified. What can be verified is that when I sectioned through the base of the neck which was still present, I found that there was a hairline fracture of the cricoid cartilate and another deeper, but still incomplete fracture, of the middle line of the thyroid cartilate and one of its wings.' He wondered if Yin was a doctor. He seemed to be following. Macarthur said to his face, becoming more technical, 'The left great horn of the thyroid was fractured and bent slightly inwards – only slightly – and the cricoid was hairline fractured on both sides – again, almost impossible to see without close examination and a glass – and the central portion, in front, was displaced backwards.'

Feiffer said, 'What killed her?'

'Asphyxia.'

'Consistent with a heart attack.'

'Yes. Assuming the heart was weak or the patient at an advanced age or in poor condition. Yes.' He looked at John Yin and thought he looked well-dressed enough for a doctor, one in private practice. Macarthur said, 'Yes, a heart attack certainly would have occurred.' He glanced back into the open coffin. Bones were less easy. He waited for the well-dressed doctor to reach the appropriate conclusion.

The Chinese in the expensive suit looked at him. His eyes were full of tears. He didn't seem to understand at all.

Macarthur said quickly, to help him, 'Asphyxia, bringing on a coronary incident of massive proportions sufficient to exhibit the gross outward signs of –' It was hopeless. The Chinese wasn't a doctor at all. He was something else. Macarthur said quickly, 'She was struck by a blow on the throat delivered at terrific speed and with terrific force that temporarily cut off her breathing, starved her brain of oxygen and, because of her age and probable history of heart trouble, stopped her heart almost instantly.' They were going to ask what had delivered the blow, man or object. Macarthur said, 'The delivery of the blow was done with, I'm guessing, the side of a hand padded in some sort of light material to avoid bruising: a glove perhaps, or simply a piece of cotton wrapped around the palm.' He saw their faces. 'She was murdered. In the text books it comes somewhere between death by throttling, mugging, and simple strangulation.' He looked down at the bones. He said softly, sad that his victory had gone professionally unremarked, 'It's what I believe the military in their Special Forces manuals call "silent killing".'

Macarthur said, Holmes playing without a Watson, 'Take my word for it: whoever did it was a real, practised, one hundred per cent expert.'

They were all the coffins of the poor or the disfigured, the coffins with the dead in them that no one wanted to see again or no one cared to see again. They were the coffins of Old Hundred Names: the eternal nameless Chinese with no one and nothing but his work and his gods to sustain him. The bodies, like Old Hundred Names himself, had come in from China. Soon the Chinese would be coming in.

3.28 a.m.: night's darkest moment.

At the open grave, in the smell of the kerosene lanterns of the poor and the lights of the sampans and junks on the harbour, touching at the peach stone he carried always in his tunic pocket as an emblem of longevity and a talisman against demons, PC Lee said softly in Cantonese, not to Feiffer but to John Yin, 'Sir . . . Sir, I don't understand what's happening at all.'

7

'A *Portuguese?*'

Auden said, 'No.'

Spencer said eagerly, 'I can do the accent! I hung around the Portuguese Seamen's Club in Nathan Road all last night and I've got the accent off pat.' They were in the post office sorting room X-raying the last of the letters for the morning's delivery. Spencer, slipping the umpteenth letter under the machine and getting, for the umpteenth time, an X-ray of a letter, said, '*Eh! Ven ventura, ven y dura!*'

That wasn't Portuguese, that was Spanish. And if a Portuguese said 'Eh!' it was for sure he had lost his citizenship long ago from watching too many Italian movies in the back streets of Rome. Auden, shaking his head, said, 'No.'

'You need another mailman beside you to keep an eye on your bag, you said so yourself.'

He hated it when Spencer started wheedling. Auden said, 'No.'

'A Portuguese from Macao. A Eurasian. Macanese Eurasians come in all complexions. I can be a Portuguese from Macao with a Swedish mother or a Danish father, or a White Russian —' White Russians weren't necessarily white. Spencer said, 'To the Chinese all Europeans look alike anyway.'

'I don't get Chinese. I get Samoans and Hawaiians —' Spencer had a little wooden case on the table near the letters. It was his make-up. He already had his mailman's uniform on.

Auden, pushing the last of his letters under the X-ray and reaching for his turban to terminate the conversation, said firmly, 'No. You've got no sense of restraint.' The mail sorters who should have been sorting the mail had a sense of restraint. They were restraining themselves from mail sorting. Downstairs in the toilets they were still playing cards and no doubt exchanging Communism and connivery with the dead-letter man. Auden said, 'No, for the last time – no.'

'An American writer getting atmosphere for his next novel.' Spencer, slipping into character, said to convince him, 'Hi, there –'

He had heard his American accent yesterday. Auden said, 'No.'

'Phil, I can't see anything from across the road! And I can't keep wandering along staring at you through the viewfinder of a camera. I have to get up close.'

He put on his beard. With it on, he felt better. Auden, shaking his beard to test the glue, said, 'No.'

Spencer said, 'You need protection.'

He needed his magnum.

'If there is someone dropping bombs in your mail-bag you need someone who can get there quickly with a fire bucket.' He saw Auden's face. 'If there was some one there right next to you he could wrench the bag physically from your back and you wouldn't need a fire bucket.' Spencer, hitting on it, said enthusiastically, 'I can be a deaf and dumb!'

'A deaf and dumb what?'

'A deaf and dumb anything!' He wasn't wheedling, he was positively grovelling. 'A deaf and dumb Portuguese –' The possibilities were unlimited. 'I could be a deaf and dumb American writer looking for atmosphere! I could be –'

He was losing ground. Auden said, 'There aren't any deaf and dumb American writers –'

'What about Helen Keller?'

Auden said, 'She's dead.'

'I could be a deaf and dumb American writer in the *tradition* of Helen Keller.' He had had a private education. He had spent his life trying not to show it off. Spencer, desperate, said, 'You don't read much, but if you did you'd be surprised to know just how many American writers really are deaf and dumb.'

Auden, wavering, said, scratching at his beard, 'Look, Bill, I know you're only offering to help out of the best motives —'

Spencer said, 'I am. I'd hate to see you get seriously hurt.'

'— but the best thing you can do is follow up the theory about the —' He tried to remember what the theory was about. '— the theory about the dead-letter man and the postcard.' If Gary Cooper was going to lie dead in the dirt it wasn't going to be side by side with a deaf and dumb Portuguese raving about the merits of American literature or scribbling sign-language notes in the dust for his next novel. Auden said encouragingly, 'What you should do if you think there's something funny about the way the dead-letter man took the Waikiki postcard, is get hold of the postcard and then take yourself off to a library some-where and read up on everything you can find about Waikiki.' That would hold him for about a week. Auden said, 'And then there's the stamps. I thought that showed a glimmer of prom-ise, the stamps line. Maybe after you've read the Waikiki bit you should find a stamp expert somewhere and —'

Spencer said, 'I pinched the postcard from the dead-letter man's office this morning.' He took it out from his pocket and held it up. It was a plain ordinary coloured postcard of the beach at Waikiki with grains of sand glued on to it. On the back it read *Funds low. Please send $500. (U.S.) Henry.* Spencer said, 'And, as a matter of fact, I had my stamp books with me in the Portuguese Club and the stamp on it is a plain, ordinary US airmail stamp.' Spencer said, deeply hurt, 'You don't want me.'

The sorting room was empty and silent. So was Spencer. Auden, seeing his face, said with an effort at sincerity, 'Bill, you drive me crazy! I can't keep an eye out all the time for some maniac who's going to drop a bomb into my mail-bag if you're constantly —' The sincerity just wouldn't stick. Auden snarled, 'You drive me out of my fucking mind drivelling about bloody stamps and bananas and T-shirts and bloody funny accents — some bugger is chucking bombs into mail-bags and all I can hear is you raving in my beard about the history of the Hong

Kong post office and the bloody price of fish and the bloody –'
Auden said, 'No!'

'If I was deaf and dumb I wouldn't say a word.'

'No.'

'We can take the radios off.' Spencer, tapping at his box of faces, said, 'I'll wear the same uniform as you –' He saw the look on Auden's face. '– not the beard or the turban – and I'll –' Spencer said, 'You can't do this alone; you need me.'

'I need my bloody *gun*!'

There was a silence. Spencer, his face slowly lighting up, said, 'You can have mine . . .' He had it in a belt holster in the small of his back. Spencer, drawing it ever so slowly and holding it out in his palm, said invitingly, 'It isn't a Python like yours and it's only got a little barrel, but it's a brand new Detective Special with the new ejection rod shroud that replaced the old open model.' It had recently been reblued. The short barrel shone in the light. Spencer said, '.38 Special, hollow-point 200-grain lead bullet with a muzzle velocity of 730 feet per second with a delivery, as they say in the James Bond movies, of a brick through a plate-glass window.'

There was a silence. There was only the sound of Auden running his tongue across his lips. Auden, his eyes glazing, said in a strange, somnambulist's voice, 'Only if it's a very small plate-glass window.' He reached out to touch it. Auden, his little hand getting all sweaty, asked politely, 'Can I touch it?'

'It isn't as good as your gun, but then you haven't got your gun. Your gun is locked up in Christopher O'Yee's drawer.' He drew back the gun from Auden's hand. Spencer said, 'Deaf and dumb. I won't say a word.' He asked quietly, 'Yes? No?' He began to close his hand around the gun. Spencer asked . . .

'All right!' He had it. It felt heavy. It felt warm. Auden said, 'All right, you've made yourself a deal!'

'You *need* a friend!'

He had one. It was a .38 calibre throwing a 200-grain bullet at 730 feet per second. Auden, shoving it deep into his pocket and shouldering his bag, said, 'OK! But deaf and dumb, OK? Deaf and bloody dumb – *all right*?'

He saw Spencer nod.

78

Auden said, 'Right!'

Spencer's hands came up and one tapped him on the shoulder to get his attention. Spencer's hand, waving in sign language, said happily, 'Good! Yes! Away we go!' He patted Auden hard on the shoulder. His hands, waving about and patting him, tapping him to get his attention, pointing, gesticulating, talking sign, said, babbling, 'We'll win! Stop us? Nothing can stop us! You and me, together: whiz, bang, wallop, how can we fail?'

Auden said softly, 'Oh, no . . .' He touched at the gun in his pocket.

The hands said, 'Gun? In pocket? Good spot for gun. Good gun. Bang, bang: big gun, good gun, my gun. Now your gun. You me – friends!'

Auden said, 'Oh, Jesus . . .' Sometimes, whatever you did, you just couldn't win.

Auden said softly, 'Oh . . .'

Gathering up his mail and his bag and shouldering it, he went towards the door of the sorting room towards the outside where it was going to be hot and, without a shadow of doubt, sometime this morning – as sure as God made little green apples – the way his luck was going he was going to be blown up or burned to cinders.

Well, that was the way it went.

There were worse things.

It was just that, with Spencer flailing happily away on his shoulder, making grunting noises and jumping up and down on the spot to get his attention, off-hand, he just couldn't quite think what they might be.

The girl's voice on the other end of the line said in Cantonese, 'Good morning, Better Business Bureau. May I help you?' She sounded fresh, young and innocent. It was 7 a.m. She sounded wide awake and, poor fool, happy to greet the day.

'This is Detective Senior Inspector O'Yee of the Yellow-thread Street Station, Hong Bay.'

'Aiiya . . . !' It was the Cantonese equivalent of Gosh.

O'Yee said in a kindly voice, 'This may sound a little silly to you, but I wonder if you might ask one of your superiors to see if he can get together a list of small businesses in the area that appear to be heavily capitalized with maybe one or two employees –'

The girl said with an Ooo, 'Oh, there are lots of those . . .'

'– that don't seem to actually produce anything, or, if they do, don't produce enough to justify their apparent capitalization and location.' He was being gentle. The world would creep up on her soon enough. O'Yee said, 'If you see what I mean . . .'

'Aaiyya . . .' She was like a rose. He could almost smell her fragrance. The girl said, 'Do you mean, like one of the offices of the Secret Services?'

O'Yee said, 'Pardon?' O'Yee said, 'Yes!'

'British, American, Communist or Nationalist Chinese, Swedish, Japanese, Australian or Libyan?'

O'Yee said, 'Communist Chinese!'

'Do you mean the secret office of the Ministry Of External Calm?'

O'Yee said, 'Yes!'

The girl said, 'Room 8, third floor, 78 Peking Road, Hong Bay.'

O'Yee said, 'Oh.' O'Yee said, 'Well, um –'

The girl said, 'Mr O'Yee the policeman!' The girl said happily, 'I was at the same school as your daughter Penelope. I was two classes ahead of her.' The girl asked fragrantly, 'Anything else I can help you with?'

O'Yee, clutching at his Thoreau, said, 'No . . . no thanks.' O'Yee said, 'Thanks very much.'

It wasn't that he was terrified, weak-kneed, acid-stomached, trembling in his boots, that worried him: that wasn't what worried him at all. Let the Ministry Of External Calm have him. Who cared?

He sighed.

He didn't matter anyway.

He was suddenly, abruptly . . .

. . . *old*.

'There's nobody here. I'm just the cleaner. They cleared out the office a week ago and now there's nobody here.'

On the phone O'Yee said, 'Room 8, third floor, 78 Peking Road, Hong Bay – right?'

There was a pause. The cleaner sounded like the sort of thickly-built, unshaven, bald-pated Chinese who, half the time, didn't know what time it was. There was a scritching sound on the line as he scratched away at his bald pate with his gnarled thick fingers. The cleaner said, 'I don't know. I can't read. It's just where I always clean today.' There was another scritching sound. The cleaner said, 'It's the Hong Kong office of the Chinese Secret Service – is that any help?' The cleaner said, 'No, that isn't any help. You already know that. Everybody knows that. Everybody's known that for years.' He was thinking and scritching. He was as thick as two short planks. Trying hard to think what time it was half the time wore him out.

The cleaner, his brain hurting with the effort, asked, 'What was it you asked me again?'

It was her. On the line Miss Fan said urgently, 'Find me!'

She got no reply.

'Christopher? Mr O'Yee? *Comrade?*'

O'Yee said tightly, 'Room 8, third floor, 78 Peking Road, Hong Bay.' O'Yee said, 'But you've moved, haven't you?'

There was a silence.

Miss Fan said, 'Have we?' There was a pause as she opened her Thoreau. Miss Fan said easily, '"Beware of all enterprises that require new clothes."' She said, '*Walden.*'

'"It takes two to speak the truth – one to speak, and another to hear."' O'Yee said firmly, '*A Week on the Concord and Merrimac Rivers.*'

'"Our life is frittered away by detail . . . Simplify, simplify!"' She said, '*Walden* again.'

'You've moved!'

'"Things do not change, we change . . ."' *Walden* yet again. The conclusion.'

'Everywhere men are in chains!' O'Yee snarled, 'God-damned Karl Marx!'

'Find me! Look hard! Seek me out!' Miss Fan said urgently, 'Find me quickly! Be firm. Be resolute. Leave nothing to chance.' She was some sort of spy. She was in the Ministry Of External Calm. She was somewhere nearby. She said suddenly, desperately, 'Christopher, please, I promise you: the future of the entire world may well depend on it.'

She was silent for a moment. Behind her, on the line, there was no sound at all.

She was close. It was a local call. She was ringing from somewhere on the island.

Miss Fan said in English, her voice cracking with strain and emotion, 'Please! I promise you this is true! Please – *Hurry!*'

All his life, except for a brief period as a child during the war when he had been evacuated to Australia, he had lived in Asia. He had been born there, as had his father and his grandfather before him. His own son had been born in Hong Kong and, like him, was going to grow up speaking Cantonese at school and English at home and, like him, wonder one day who he was.

It was a little after 7.30 a.m. and Feiffer, sitting in his car at the terminus of Hong Bay Beach Road and Yellowthread Street, sat watching the boat people in Wharf Cove and turning his cigarette over and over in his fingers.

In the cove the boat people were up and about their business on their junks and sampans, their cooking fires rising as blue smudges against the clear cloudless sky and the still, brilliant water. There were hundreds of them, their boats all moored or lashed tightly together, going nowhere, forming walkways and ramps, streets going from one hull to another, their washing hung from mast to mast, brightly coloured and chaotic, moving in the slight morning breeze in from the sea.

All their lives they would spend on their boats, coming in to the land only for their deaths and burials. They were the Tanka: the people of the sea – he watched as a girl in a wide rattan Tanka hat sculled past the nearest of the mass of boats and, not glancing at all at the shore, manœuvred her sampan to some unknown, important destination among the masts and the washing.

Behind them, overshadowing them each morning as the day

began, was Hong Kong. Behind Hong Kong, behind the mountains that hid it, but there – always there – was the centre of the world, the Middle Kingdom, the centre of Heaven: *China*.

He had absolutely no idea at all what was happening with the bodies, no notion: despite all the languages he spoke, all the knowledge he had, all his family's life-long understanding of the secret lines and beliefs that held Hong Kong and China together, he had not the faintest glimmer of what was happening with the bodies.

He knew no one who would know. Feiffer, looking down at the burned-away cigarette in his hand, said softly to no one, 'I don't know.' The girl in the sampan, having delivered whatever was in the sampan that had been so important, or having picked up something important, came back into view from behind a boat sculling at the single stern oar with new urgency. She was making a living. Feiffer, watching her, said, shaking his head, 'What are you going to do when the Communists come?'

She would prosper. The Chinese always prospered. It was something deep down in their systems. They did not allow the world to beat them; they, in their particular idiom, slaving through the world, in the end became the masters of that world.

Behind the mountains, the eight hundred million Chinese who called themselves Communists would also prosper. They would change, cease being Communists as they had ceased being Stalinists and, prospering, becoming Chinese again. They would change, alter, adapt, vary the world according to the way the world was – and they would prosper.

Learning without thought is labour lost; thought without learning is perilous. He was beginning to sound like Christopher O'Yee. Feiffer, crushing out the cigarette in the ashtray by the steering wheel, said irritably, 'Who do I know? If I don't know what's happening – if I don't understand it, who do I know who would?'

There was no one. If John Yin of The Society For Neglected Bones did not know and he himself did not know, there was no one.

Watching the girl about her business, seeing the boats and the washing and the fires, feeling the pulsing of their lives, Feiffer, his eyes still on the Tankas, took up the newspaper on the seat beside him and, not looking at it, folded it over on his lap. His eyes wandered to the text and the photographs and the headlines telling of the latest Sino-British negotiations on the future of Hong Kong.

He paused. In Hong Kong there were over sixty Chinese and English language newspapers produced every week. The one he had on his lap was in Chinese. Each day, along with a newspaper in English, he read it without noticing what language either was in.

He should have known what was happening with the coffins!

He should have known someone who did!

They were the poor, the disfigured, the ordinary people of this world and someone, somewhere, was cutting them into pieces like meat and strewing them in the ground like the secret bone caches of dogs.

He should have known what it meant!

Feiffer, crushing the folded newspaper in his hands, said in total, angry frustration, 'God damn it!'

He should have known someone.

He glanced at the newspaper.

He looked down at the column of characters in front of him and the photographs. At the boats, the girl in the sampan was gone, off on her business, surviving, prospering, not once looking up or back to the Hong Kong that, on three sides surrounded every aspect of her life.

He looked hard at the characters.

The story and photographs in the newspaper were about a man called Howell. The photograph showed a tall, balding man outside a hotel on Peak Street.

In one of the photographs he was holding in his hand what looked like a set of gleaming sharp acupuncture needles. With his other hand he was pointing at them and grinning.

Both the set of needles and Howell, the story around the photograph said, had come to Hong Kong only yesterday.

It was an unctious, sympathetic story, full of praise for the

84

man's achievements and contribution in the fields of medicine and international co-operation.

He was an American, a surgeon. He had arrived in the Colony only yesterday.

He had come from China where he had been working in a hospital there.

He had come direct from the Military Hospital where he had been working to the Sumatran Lela Hotel on Peak Street before he continued his journey onwards to his home in America.

He had come from Canton.

'The Soong family private cemetery off Singapore Road, the servants' section.'

'Yes?'

'Win Kai Sun, male, deceased China five months ago. No living relatives.'

'Yes?' The Captain, writing it down in his pad in a booth in the call-box section of the Hong Bay Telephone Company on Wyang Street, asked, 'When?'

'Daylight.' The voice at the other end of the line, speaking Mandarin, said quietly, 'Now.'

'Yes?'

The voice said, 'You'll see. When you open it you'll see as before.' The voice said, 'End of message.' He sounded military.

'Understood.' In the booth, the Captain in charge of the Resurrection Squad, with no show of emotion and no questions, said crisply, 'Understood.' If the man at the other end of the line had any rank the Captain did not acknowledge it.

Still standing in the booth he took a small map from his pocket and began to consult it.

He was unafraid. He knew all around the call-box section and at the door to the street, his squad were there, out of sight, protecting him.

In the booth, he put the tip of his finger onto the junction of Singapore Street and Yellowthread Street on the unfolded map and, carefully, began to figure the safest route.

85

8

In the lobby of the Sumatran Lela Hotel on Peak Street, Doctor John Howell said expansively, 'You always thought Lela was a girl, right?' He was a balding, bright-eyed Texan who, even when he wasn't wearing a Stetson was wearing a Stetson. He had that glow only the healthy and the rich have. Judging by his tailored shirt and slacks and the way he held himself, he was both. Howell, taking Feiffer authoritatively by the arm and leading him into the empty Lantaka bar near the reception desk, said, 'No, not so. It's a cannon.' The walls of the bar were lined with a display of Sumatran cannons – Lelas and Lantakas, little bronze swivel guns varying from plain tubes about a foot long to an ornate dragon-muzzled monster eight feet from cascabel to dragon nose. Howell, gazing at them wistfully for a moment, said, 'They're the fore and aft cannons of the old Malay and Sumatran prahus and pirate boats. Some of them date back to the sixteenth century.' He went to touch one, but, like all the display, it was chained to the wall and just out of reach. Howell, touching at his chin with the tip of his manicured index finger, said pleasantly, 'You may not believe this as a civilized Britisher from an overcrowded island, but where I come from you don't need a police permit to collect things like that.'

The island Feiffer came from was Hong Kong. In Hong Kong the island wasn't overcrowded, it was teeming. Feiffer said equally pleasantly, 'How long were you studying acupuncture in Canton?' He asked, 'It was at the Military Hospital there, wasn't it?'

He hadn't asked the point of the interview. It didn't concern him. He hadn't done anything wrong. Ever. Howell said, 'Eight weeks.' The cannons had all been cast in the Spanish style using the lost-wax process. Each one of them was unique. 'I'm an anaesthetist. It was a sort of two-way traffic. They wanted to learn about our new Western techniques and I wanted to learn about their old ones.' Howell, grinning, said, 'Good old Nixon and the Open Door Policy. It was no trouble at all.' During the war the Japanese had melted down half the Lelas in the Malay archipelago for the bronze. It was becoming a connoisseur's hobby, collecting Eastern cannons. 'You know they used to use cannons as currency in this part of the world and some of them – the larger ones with cascabels –' Howell said, '– the cascabel is the knob on the breech end – some of them were used as fertility symbols. Infertile women used to think that if they sat astride one of them the demon that fired the charge would grant them children.' He asked abruptly, 'A Detective Chief Inspector: how many ranks higher than a sergeant is that?'

'Three or four.' Feiffer, turning the man gently around to face him, asked, 'Is there anything you can tell me about the hospital?'

'Like what?'

'Like anything at all.'

'No.' The cannons fascinated him. Howell, turning to look Feiffer carefully up and down as if there was something about him he was considering, said shaking his head, 'No, it's just a normal, slightly under-equipped non-specialist general hospital.' He thought for a moment, 'It's not military, if that's what you're asking. That appears to be just a convenient way for the staff to requisition equipment and for the Chinese administrative system to allocate it to them. It deals mainly with the middle echelons of Party members from the city and the surrounding province of Kwantung, but I never saw any evidence of military activity.' He said, thinking about it, 'No. Most of the medical staff told me that during the Cultural Revolution they were all sent off to be carpenters and night soil-carriers and paddy-field workers to learn about the lives of the struggling masses. If they had been in the military I think they would have avoided that – wouldn't you?'

'Yes.'

He was back gazing at the cannons. Howell said, 'That big one with the dragon muzzle, that's a rare one. It was cast at the Meningkabau foundry in Sumatra. There's only one other like it in a recognized collection and that's in the Singapore Museum.' He turned to glance again at Feiffer, again looking him up and down, again summing him up or considering something. Howell said, 'I noticed when you came in you carry a Colt Airweight in a belt holster –' His mind was not on what he was saying. Howell said suddenly, intensely, 'If I could get hold of a dragon-muzzled Lela here and take it back with me to Houston there are a lot of cannon freaks like me who wouldn't stop drooling over it for a month.' He sighed, 'Money isn't the problem. On overcrowded islands it's always the paperwork.'

'There's a train-track spur somewhere near the hospital. Did you ever see it?'

'No.'

'What about the mortuary? Did you ever have any call to go in?'

'As an anaesthetist?' Howell, smiling, said, 'No, the patients who were in there were already far enough under without my help.' He paused for a moment, thinking. 'The mortuary. Is that what you're interested in?'

'Possibly.'

'Why?'

'I can't say.'

'When? Recently? During my time?'

'Possible. Possibly a week ago or thereabouts.' He thought of Owens and his trains. The world was full of eccentrics. Or maybe it was the world that was eccentric and train spotters and cannon freaks were the normal ones. Feiffer, drawing a breath, said patiently, 'Look, I can't tell you what the enquiry concerns. I don't even know what I really want you to tell me. It's a long shot, but something awful is happening and I just thought maybe you –'

Howell said, 'There's a dragon-mouthed Lela for sale here in Hong Kong. The price is reasonable, but I can't apply for a police permit to export it.'

It was hopeless. Feiffer said, yielding, 'You don't need a permit. Provided you're going to export it, all you do is get the owner or the dealer to send it out to your aircraft under Customs seal and they can put it on your plane for you. If you don't need a permit at your end you can then simply take it off the plane and do what you like with it.' Feiffer, turning to go, said, 'OK? You don't need a permit, just the previous owner here in Hong Kong.'

'It's important – whatever it is you don't want to ask me directly, is it? About the hospital?'

'Yes.'

Howell said suddenly, 'The present owner doesn't have a permit for it. The present owner has had it in a cupboard since the year Dot and there's no way the present owner can approach the police to get a permit for it without telling the police he hasn't already got a permit for it.' He waited. Touching Feiffer gently on the arm to hold him, Howell said, 'What is it you want to know about the Canton Military Hospital and why?'

'*Someone is butchering bodies in the bloody mortuary there and sending them into Hong Kong in sealed coffins and I haven't got the faintest idea why!*'

'I see.'

'*Do you know anything?*'

Howell said with a smile, 'Do you smoke?'

'Yes. Why?'

Howell said, 'I can't tell you anything. Everything that may have happened in China is covered by (a) the State Department not wanting me to talk out of turn about anything that might reflect badly on the Chinese and (b) my common courtesy and gratitude stemming from the fact that while I was there I was treated with great respect.' He touched at his chin again with his finger and then nipped at the point of his tongue as if there was a speck of tobacco caught there. Howell said, 'Smoking is so bad for you. I gave up smoking while I was in Canton using acupuncture and I can honestly say I felt a whole lot better for it and I don't have any funny ideas any more.' He went on before Feiffer could say anything. 'Smoking makes you imagine funny things. There was an orderly in the hospital, for example, who committed suicide while I was there, shot himself, and, since, as you've gathered, I'm interested in things that go bang in the night I asked one of the senior doctors what sort of gun he had used.' Howell said quickly, conscious of his position, 'I don't shoot guns myself, I just collect them.' He saw Feiffer screw up his face in incomprehension. 'He told me it was some sort of old rusty piece from the Nationalist days: you know some sort of old Browning automatic or Belgian Annihilator or something that hasn't been made for donkey's years . . .' He gazed at the dragon-mouthed cannon. 'He told me he saw the ejected shell case near the man's head.' Howell said, 'Funny thing smoking. It makes you imagine people saying things that later they'd deny ever having said.' Howell, glancing at Feiffer, said evenly, 'It was a brand new, shiny empty cartridge case, in Canton, in China, in the Canton Military Hospital with the letters W-W on the base.' He said, 'That, in case you don't know it, stands for American, unobtainable in China, Winchester-Western ammunition.' Howell said, 'I thought that was what he told me, but since I was smoking at the time, and thinking of Lelas that I can't have because the owner doesn't have a permit, I probably got it wrong.'

Feiffer said quietly, 'I can issue the present owner a permit.'

'I thought you could.'

Feiffer asked, 'When do you leave the Colony?'

'Tonight.'

'I can issue you a note saying the police are aware of the existence of the weapon, but an expert advised us that it was inoperable and for the purposes of decoration only.'

Howell said, 'It is. It's unique. If I don't buy it, one day, when he needs money, he's going to sell it to some lunatic, who's going to fire it and blow it to hell, or, when the Chinese take this place over, it'll end up melted down for the bronze to make souvenirs.'

Feiffer said, 'I don't have an expert on Lelas on hand.'

Howell said, 'Yes, you do.'

'When? When did this happen in the hospital?' He knew the answer. Feiffer said, 'A week ago – am I right?'

'Yes.'

Howell said, 'Thank you very much. I know you're putting yourself out for me and bending the law, but it really is very important to me.' He was not that much of a lunatic. Howell said, 'It really would be such a pity to see something worthwhile end up as nothing.'

'Why did he kill himself?'

Howell said, 'Did he? Where did he get the modern ammunition?' Howell said, 'Did he? My friend on the staff said he'd shot himself slightly behind and below the right ear, going upwards.' Howell said, 'Odd that – since my friend told me he knew for a fact that the orderly had always been left-handed.' Howell said, 'No, I never saw the train-track spur near the hospital, but it's funny you should ask – it was just there, near one of the trains, that the man shot himself.' Howell said, 'But I imagined all this and if you asked at the hospital now they'd deny it. They were denying it the next morning.' Howell said, 'But then that's life. Even in a Communist society there are the important people and the unimportant people and he, the suicide, in the hospital pecking order, considering where he worked, was fairly unimportant from a medical point of view.' He gazed longingly at the Lela on the wall and thought of his own. His own was finer. Howell said with real gratitude, 'Thank you very much indeed.'

Feiffer said, almost afraid to ask, 'Where did the orderly usually work in the hospital?'

He hadn't given up smoking by acupuncture in the hospital. If he had he would have been wearing a stub in his right earlobe. Howell said, smiling, 'In the mortuary. He was the post-mortem assistant. Not very bright and, as a rule, messy, but if you're going to put your work in the ground who cares what sort of job you do on it?' Howell said, 'He was the one who chopped up corpses for autopsies and sewed them back again after the pathologist had finished.' He said, 'Let me have a cigarette, would you?' He said quietly, gazing at the cannon, 'Funny sort of job, neither fish nor fowl – not so much a paramedic as, well, more like a – a butcher.'

Under the invisible Stetson there was a lot more than just Texas Prime. Howell, lighting his cigarette from Feiffer's match and drawing in the smoke, said, shaking his head, 'But I didn't say any of this. I was still smoking at the time and thinking about cannons.' He said, 'That gun up there on the wall was made in the Meningkabau foundry and so was the one the Singapore Museum has got. The one I'm getting today was made somewhere else – in Atcheh district.' He seemed happy. 'That's even better. That's the only one known from there.' He said suddenly, very seriously, 'Thank you for what you've done. It may sound a little stupid to you, but it really is something worth saving.' He asked, 'Can you understand that?'

It was the morning of the second day. It wasn't much, but it was something. At least it was *something*.

Feiffer said, nodding, 'Yes. Yes, I can understand that.' He glanced at Howell's face for a moment gazing at his cannons and, reaching inside his coat for his list of Headquarters numbers, went quickly towards the reception desk in the lobby to ring someone in the Firearms Branch to save something someone somewhere, at least, thought was worth saving.

'Headquarters Station, People's Police, Canton.'

He was calling from a public phone in Khartoum Street. He knew they listened to the pips. He knew they counted the coins.

There was a silence. They knew he was calling from Hong Kong.

Feiffer said in Cantonese, 'This is Detective Chief Inspector Feiffer of the Royal Hong Kong Police calling for your Serious Crimes Section. Connect me with the senior Homicide officer.'

There was a silence.

Feiffer said, 'Hullo? Are you there?'

They knew.

The line to China, abruptly, went dead.

'Military Intelligence Unit, Victoria Barracks, Duty Officer, speaking.'

'Brigadier Smith here-yah.'

'Yes, Brigadier Smith, sir?'

O'Yee had his thumb in his mouth. A plum would have been better but he was too nervous to go out and buy one. He was also too morally fragile to talk to any more fourteen-year-olds at Better Business. O'Yee said, mumbling, thumb in mouth, talking not to the phone but to the blotter on his desk, 'Actually, that's Brigadier-*General* Smith –'

'Sah!'

'– Smith-*Horsely* –'

'Very sorry, Sah!'

'*VC*.'

The Duty Officer said in a gasp, 'Oh my God!'

'– of the Promotions Board.'

He heard a gulp.

'– thought I might amble over and have a shufty at the general balls-up around your little show –' It was a great laconic English accent. It was so laconic the hard part was not to fall asleep in the middle of it. O'Yee said, yawning, 'Bit of a bloody cock-up over at the Secret Service on um Street . . .' He waited. He asked, 'Are you getting this, young fella me lad or are you . . .'

The voice was very young. It was getting younger by the moment. The voice said, 'Yes, sir! The SIS on Empress Of India Street, yes, sir! Lieutenant Carr, sir!'

Groveller. O'Yee said, 'Young pup, it's Market Lane where the SIS have their Station!' He made an Harrumph sound. O'Yee, pulling at his walrus moustache, roared, 'Don't you pretend to know something if you don't know something!'

'Sir, it's Empress Of India Street. I was just over there myself yesterday and –'

'And now they've changed it! My God, man, why the hell do you think they call it the Secret Service?' O'Yee, relenting, said with a grunt, 'Still, I expect you've got all sorts of good bloody connections in Staff and you're rich and you'll make Colonel whatever happens.' He muttered, 'In my day –'

'No, sir, I don't know anyone at all!' Lieutenant Carr said obediently, 'Yes, sir, Market Lane as from today, yes, sir, I'll make a note of it!' He asked meekly, 'Phone number?'

'That's the same.' He waited. O'Yee said, 'Well? What is it?'

'Five-nine seven eight two one, *Sah*!'

'*Jolly* good!'

'Thank you, sah!'

O'Yee said, 'Thank you.' At the other end of the line there was a subaltern contemplating suicide. He couldn't leave him like that.

O'Yee, all heart, said encouragingly, 'Have a nice day.'

He was in the same position as Jim Hawkins had been with Long John Silver: hit a handicapped person in the middle of the street and everyone was against you. Auden, flexing his fists, his beard and turban quivering with restraint, said with an awful grin fixed on his face for the benefit of passers-by, 'Deliver the mail!'

'Erk, hmmph-ha, erk.' That meant, along with the head-shaking, pointing and gesticulating that the mail he carried was the second mail of the day – 'Erk, hhm-ha, hm-ha' – and that the second mail of the day wasn't going to be delivered until the first mail of the day had been delivered. 'Err-ka.' Regulations.

Auden said, '*Look –!*' He wasn't delivering mail at all. He was thinking. You could tell. Auden, pausing at the junction of Jade Street and Soochow Street, still grinning as a party of fourteen-year-old Chinese schoolgirls twittered past on their way to flower-arranging or blossoming or whatever they did, said to Spencer at the end of his patience, '*Look –!*'

The girls did. Auden, reaching for his throat, said, 'Listen, you dummy –!

Spencer touched at his ears and mouth and shrugged. He went, 'Errk . . .'

The girls went, 'Ohhh . . .'

Auden said, 'Look . . .' He smiled at the girls.

The girls didn't smile back.

Auden said gently, touching Spencer on the shoulder and digging his fingers in deep, 'Look, Bill, listen –'

One of the girls said in English, 'He's *deaf*!'

They were from a convent school. The nuns had told them all about men who were as blond and as handsome as Spencer. They had also told them to be gentle to injured things. The girls, consumed with lust and motherhood, said in unison, 'And he's mute, poor man!' It was an old English missionary order. They had heard what the Sepoys had done to the English nuns in India. The head girl said as an order, 'Leave him alone you horrible Indian!'

Auden said – Auden said – Auden said in Cantonese, with a smile, 'Please go away girls or you'll be late for school.' He took his hand away from Spencer's shoulder. Spencer continued grimacing. He had an audience. Spencer said with a sad, slow movement of his hand, 'Errk, hmm, erk . . .'

The girls said, 'Ohh . . .'

Auden said, 'Why don't you all just –' Auden said, 'Get to school!'

The head girl said, 'My father's a judge.' She nuzzled up next to the poor Quasimodo to protect him from the mob. The head girl, narrowing her eyes, said, 'Touch him one more time and I'll scream.'

One of the other girls said, 'So will I.' She also nuzzled.

Spencer patted her on the head.

Auden said, 'Listen –!' Auden said, 'OK, I'm sorry. I won't do it again!' Auden, staring at Spencer with a terrible stare, said carefully, quietly, kindly, 'Well, Sahib, perhaps we should stop pretending to these poor girls that we don't like each other and get on delivering the mail.' He said, 'My goodness, what would your Mother Superior say if you were late?'

The other nuzzler said, 'My father is with the Tax Office.' She watched as Spencer gently pushed her to one side and reaching into his bag, withdrew the coloured postcard of Waikiki to show her. The girl said, taking him by his free hand and squeezing it, 'Oh, yes, that's pretty, isn't it? Pretty.'

The man of a thousand faces said, 'Erk.' He looked happy. He put the corner of the postcard to his lips and began sucking it.

Auden said in a snarl, 'Spencer –!'

'Pretty . . .' Both the girls nuzzled simultaneously. Spencer, bouncing up and down in happiness, said to the other girls, 'Erk! Erk!' It was an invitation to the nuzzle. They didn't need to be asked twice.

'Spencer –!'

95

The head girl said, 'Shut your face!'

Spencer said joyfully, 'Erk, erk, humphh!' Out of the corner of his eye he watched as a giant tough-looking Polynesian on the other side of the road ducked into a doorway out of sight. A little behind him, an equally tough-looking short Melanesian also ducked out of sight and, behind him again, there was another figure – someone he knew well.

Auden said in the lowest of low voices, 'Spencer, one of these days I'm going to do something I'll have to swing for.' He began walking away with his mail.

Spencer, his eyes still on the little procession of people across the road, all hiding at once, said to the girls, 'Erk!' He gave them all a kindly pat on the head. He sucked absently at the corner of the postcard. It tasted odd.

Across the road, behind the Polynesian and the Melanesian, he saw the dead-letter man touch at something under his shirt to check it was still there. Spencer, shepherding the girls on their way, said to thank them, 'Erk . . . ah . . . erk . . .' He turned to follow Auden on his delivery. He couldn't resist it. He knew they watched him go.

He was a poor deaf mute down on his luck.

He produced a limp.

'Universal Amusements.'

Surely they didn't still use things like passwords. O'Yee said, 'British Secret Service, Hong Bay Station? Put me on to someone in your surveillance section.'

'Universal Amusements.'

O'Yee said, 'Hullo? Hullo?'

'Universal Amusements.'

O'Yee said, 'Hullo? Are you there?' They still used passwords. O'Yee said, 'Look, I'm not with the Service, but I'm–'

'Universal Amusements.'

O'Yee said, 'Um –' He heard a click on the line. O'Yee, his every word being recorded, said, *'Um –!'*

'Good morning, may I help you?' It was a man's voice, speaking Cantonese. They were keeping him on the line. The voice said, changing to English, 'Yes? How may I assist?'

He heard another click.

The voice said cautiously, 'Swordstick.' The voice waited for the counter word.

'Um –'

That wasn't it.

O'Yee, hearing more clicks, said in a lather of sweat, 'Oh, I, um – I just – oh, I –' He said, 'Hullo? Oh, I –' O'Yee said in a stroke of pure genius, *'Excalibur!'*

There was a click. The voice said quickly in English, 'Yes?'

O'Yee said, 'British Secret Service, Hong Bay Station?'

The voice said quickly, 'Yes.' The voice said with concern, 'Is that you, Harrington?'

O'Yee said in a whisper, 'Yes.' O'Yee said quietly, quickly, 'I'll get back to you. Is that you, Ian?'

'No, this is George.'

'Ah.' The clicking had stopped. 'George . . .' It was the merest of whispers.

'Yes?'

O'Yee said darkly, 'I'll get back to you.'

There was a pause. They were waiting.

O'Yee said efficiently, 'Message timed at 08.52 hours.' He listened. The clicking had stopped. They were happy.

He hung up.

In the public booth at the Hong Bay Telephone Company building in Wyang Street Miss Fan hung up.

The government of the world I live in was not framed, like that in Britain, in after-dinner conversations over the wine.

Thoreau. She put the open hardback copy of his works back into her voluminous leather bag.

O'Yee's line was busy and she had not been able to get through.

She had a short-barrelled Hi-Standard .22 automatic pistol in the bottom of the bag and, by it, a box of fifty subsonic hollow-point cartridges and a screw-on silencer: a killer's kit.

Time is but the stream I go a-fishing in.

She had never heard of the man Thoreau before this.

On balance, she thought him idle and decadent.

Find me!

Find the new office of the Ministry of External Calm in Hong Kong.

Find me.

Zipping up the bag and placing it carefully by her hand on the little table in the booth, thoughtfully, she began dialling O'Yee's number to try him again.

9

In Shanghai, before the war, the Communists besieging the city had employed killers to deliver the heads of the Nationalist Chinese to their families to sow terror. Or, depending on who recounted the story or in what history you read it, it had been the Nationalists who were the killers and their victims Communists, or patriots and their killers Japanese, or just ordinary Chinese and the plot had been created by the Europeans who ran the place.

It had happened during a war that had lasted over ten years and claimed over five million lives.

It was inconceivable that something like that was happening now.

At the junction of Icehouse Street and Hong Bay Beach Lane, all the traffic was stopped to let a funeral procession pass by on its way towards the resettlement area off Cat Street. Coming from Icehouse Street, wending their way past and between the stopped cars, the white-gowned mourners and senior sons of the deceased man formed a vanguard ahead of the brocade-draped bier and the lines of professional mourners, the bands and, bringing up the rear, street children carrying placard-like brooms to sweep away the evil spirits.

It was a large and opulent funeral: passing across the intersection he saw all the paper replicas of everything the dead man had had in life: bundles of crudely printed replica paper

money, paper effigies of many servants, his wives and con-
cubines, his cars, a beautifully wrought tissue-paper replica of
a fishing or pleasure junk in full sail and, carried by the
professional funeral paper-maker himself, a wonderful, self-
supporting model of a mansion complete with crêpe trees and
silver paper streams meandering through paper gardens. It
would all be burned for the dead man to take with him to
Western Heaven in order to enjoy the fruits of his time on
Earth. Feiffer, lighting a cigarette from the lighter in his
dashboard, turned off the engine of his car to wait.

It was the funeral of a very wealthy man: a merchant. In the
brocade-covered coffin there would be the wizened corpse of
an old man wearing jade rings and amulets surrounded by —
tucked carefully within his winding sheets — talismans and
bribes and charms to guarantee his eternal and continuing
position as a person of importance.

He was not like the dogmeat or the dried bones they had
found in the coffins of the poor — he was someone. No doubt,
to further please the guardians of the next world, his undertaker would have carefully stuck a long fingernail on the little
finger of his left hand and put the hand upon scrolls of great
beauty and antiquity so he might be taken as a scholar. The
coffin, carried by professional coffin-bearers, judging by the
strain they took on their shoulders, weighed nothing. The dead
man had grown old with care and attention and simply faded
away at a great age until, day by day, his life became less
distinguishable from death and his final demise had come as a
gentle, welcome sigh at the end of a very long life.

At the intersection, he saw PC Lee holding the traffic back as
the funeral passed by. Feiffer had known him a very long time
and he gazed at his face to read what was there.

What was there was a Chinese policeman with no expression on his face holding back the traffic for the funeral of a
man who had been more than him in life and, forever, would
be more than him or any of his family in death. He saw Lee see
him. Lee was nothing more than the statue of a policeman
doing his duty. He saw Lee raise his hand to his cap in the
faintest of salutes.

At least one of the dogmeat corpses — that of Mrs Ping — had been murdered by an expert. At least one of the dogmeat corpses – Hwa Cheuk Kuen, a little better class of dogmeat, but still, compared with the merchant crossing the intersection, dogmeat – had been dragged from his repository, his coffin crowbarred open, his body violated, and his remains weighed down with chains and dumped like offal in the harbour.

The tail end of the funeral was passing. It had had not three, but seven bands playing a mixture of Western and Chinese music to see it on its way and frighten off the evil spirits that attended all passings. It was on its way to a prepared marble tomb – it would be safe.

In his car, Feiffer stubbed out his cigarette and started the engine. He saw Lee go to the traffic control box on Icehouse Street and turn the mechanism back on to restart the traffic flow.

In Shanghai, after the war, after all the besieging was over and the terror all finished, the Europeans had slunk away like beaten curs and never returned. He knew – he had been there.

He saw Lee's face watching him. He had known Lee a very long time and he thought he knew how he thought and what he believed. He had seen Lee in the pauper's cemetery when they had dug up the bones and found parts missing. He thought he knew him.

He did not know him at all.

He saw him watching from the pavement, first, the funeral disappearing up Icehouse Street, and then, the traffic flow, and then Feiffer himself.

Lee's eyes held his. Again, there was the faintest, courteous salute. Lee's shoulders were held tight. His hand, by his polished revolver holster, was shaking. In the sound of the traffic and the fading bands from the rich man's funeral, only Lee's mouth moved silently, his eyes hard and glittering, his hand still shaking.

Lee said soundlessly in Cantonese, for all he was and his family was and what was being done to people like him and them, 'Do something.'

It was an order. It was something so long ago, in Shanghai

and all the other places the Europeans had held sway in Asia, had never happened.

Lee, rubbing at his elbow with his hand, beginning to shake all over, said with his shoulders trembling, all the respect and salutes forgotten, 'You! Please! *Do something about this!*'

His real estate business was suffering. It was of no importance. He had not slept nor shaved nor changed his clothes and his fawn suit was crumpled and smelled of perspiration.

It was of no importance.

Ping Kit-Ling, Kwan Ting Nam, and, even though the Society had had only a passing interest in him, Hwa Cheuk Kuen: they were the matters of importance.

In the fireproof vaults in The Society For Neglected Bones office in Khartoum Street, John Yin, hunched over a carved table at his scrolls and records, rubbed at his face. He touched at the inside pocket of his coat and took out a gold Parker pen. There was no paper to write on in the vault, only parchment and silk. He put the pen back and, moistening the ink block on the table in front of him, picked up a wooden-handled Chinese calligraphy brush.

Ping Kit-Ling, Kwan Ting Nam . . . Hwa Cheuk Kuen – the wrote all their names in careful formal script and looked at them.

Ping Kit-Ling . . .

Kwan Ting Nam . . .

Hwa Cheuk Kuen . . .

Nobodies. People with nobody in this world and, in the next, nothing.

They were the Society's people: the poor and unimportant, the heirs of Old Hundred Names – the eternal Chinese, perspirers and slaves through life who had saved cent by cent to pay the oldest society in the world – two thousand years old when the Caesars ruled in Europe – to do nothing more than protect their bones and bodies in death.

They had nothing in common. They had died weeks, months, years apart and they had nothing in common – nothing between them – but the fact that they had died.

His business was suffering.

His business could go to hell.

Putting the brush down and steepling his fingers under his chin, Yin, smelling the smell of his own sweat, stared down at the names.

He had not known any of them. In life, they were not the sort of people he would have known.

Ping Kit-Ling, Kwan Ting Nam, Hwa Cheuk Kuen.

He rubbed at his face.

The Communists would have Hong Kong in a few years. In a few years, without a murmur of dissent from the British, they would march in and take it all and the only question in the minds of all the Chinese who lived in the place would be how best to prosper under them.

Only the Nationalists would resist it and the Nationalists, since 1949, had been confined to the island of Taiwan and even if they decided to resist it – to put their supporters out on the streets to riot – it would be the British who would put them down with police and troops before they went and the Communists would not have to lift a finger.

Somewhere, in rotting bits and bones, someone had some ghastly assemblage of human parts for no reason at all.

Somewhere, someone had taken the promises the Society had made to the poor and the unimportant and smashed them all to pieces.

Somewhere, someone –

For no reason at all –

Ping Kit-Ling.

Kwan Ting Nam.

Hwa Cheuk Kuen.

He had been educated at the Harvard Business School. With this, he might as well have been educated on the moon.

In the vault, surrounded by the scrolls, the calligraphy, the ink, brushes and the hopelessness of it all, John Yin, his business suffering, said hopelessly, angrily, furiously in English, 'God shit it! God damn *shit it!*'

He had no idea at all what was happening.

He knew how many public and private cemeteries there were in Hong Kong. There were twenty-three.

He knew how many of the poor and the dispossessed the Society in its antiquity was responsible for.

There were thousands.

He looked at his own calligraphy. He did not spend enough time on it. Instead he spent time on his business.

'God fucking shit it!'

It was all in English. There, in that place surrounded by the things he truly believed in, he would never have sworn in Chinese.

He smelled of sweat and neglect.

Alone, in that room, his trained and educated mind useless for the things that alone, for his race, were truly important, he put his hands gently to his face and, shaking his head in total, utter hopelessness, silently, began to despair.

In Chungking Road Mrs Hwa had stood for a very long time in the street looking at her car. From the early morning, before dawn, she had thought and planned to drive the car to the Taoist temple to pray for her husband's spirit and his quiet rest in heaven.

He was not in heaven. His body and his bones were incomplete and he was in limbo, his ghost roaming and shouting in terrible, lost terror.

He was an awful, headless ghost – he was the stuff of children's nightmares.

By the car, touching at it, running her hand back and forth across the fender, she bit her lip until the blood flowed.

Her thoughts went nowhere. They were as solid, as inanimate as the car.

Her eyes were dull, like a dead man's.

Standing there, as people in the street avoided her in silence, she kept running her hand back and forth across the shining black fender.

In his office Yin's phone rang. It was Kan of Kan's Western Heaven Coffin Repository. Yin said, 'Yes?'

He waited. He could hear the man fighting to get his breath.

Yin said again, urgently, 'Yes? John Yin here. Yes?'

He had seen them. They were his last moments on Earth and there were things to be arranged. Mr Kan said again, puffing, 'This is Kan of the Western Heaven Coffin Repository I know where they are – the ones violating the dead.' He said quickly before Yin could react, 'I want your vow that my body will lie undisturbed and the Society will oversee my funeral and, after three years, the disposition and permanent care of my bones.' He was an old man. His breath, in his lungs, was like a sparrow's. Kan said violently, 'I want your vow!'

'Where are you?' There was no second phone in the Society's office. Yin, gripping hard at the receiver, demanded, 'Where are you?'

'I want your vow!'

'You have made your own arrangements.'

'My arrangements are no longer good! I have no relatives, no one.' Kan said urgently, 'I have spent my life in good works and in the service of others. I have received no rewards for it. I have merely earned sufficient for my needs and I have nothing set aside for the unexpected. I am an old man. I expected nothing more than to die and be buried properly. And now that cannot happen and I want your vow that the Society will protect me!'

He had seen them. He knew where they were. Yin, fighting for control, said calmly, 'Tell me what you know. Tell me what you know.' Everything Kan had planned for his death was now no good because the place he had chosen to be buried was now no longer safe. Yin said quickly, realizing, 'Where? Which cemetery? Are they there now?'

'Yes.'

'Tell me where you are!'

'You must find me a new grave. A tomb. You have tombs. You have places set aside for the officials of the Society. I know that. There are rumours. I know you have special places.' Kan, his voice rising, said, 'Your tomb! I want your promise that my bones will lie in your own personal tomb and be tended and cared for by the members of your own family!'

He had made no such arrangements. Yin said quickly, 'Yes. You have my vow.'

'I have seen them. I know who they are.'

'*You have my vow!*'

'*Ta chia tu shih ming, pan tien pu yu jên.*' Mr Kan, translating the Mandarin for him, said sadly in Cantonese, 'Our destinies have been set with no reference to our wishes at all.' He looked out from the phone booth he was calling from at the bottom of the private road leading to Soong's private cemetery and saw death coming towards him. Mr Kan said, 'They are at Soong's where my own grave plot was laid aside for me by Mr Soong many years ago.' He said without fear, 'I have seen them and they have seen me and I am too old to run and because of who they are there is nothing to be gained by running but a little time . . .' His voice seemed to be drifting away. Mr Kan said –

'Who are they? What do they want? *What are they doing with the coffins?*'

'They are in the servants' section.' Mr Kan said, sure of Yin's vow, 'It is the poor of this world. It is never, never the rich and powerful.' His voice tightened. 'They will come. I know they will.' Mr Kan said suddenly, 'Please, please do not hang up to call the police. I promise you I will hang up on you a moment before they arrive – I promise you will not be known.' His voice and breath were quickening. Mr Kan said, 'Please, please, spend the last few moments with me talking of things I have spent my life about!' He said, trying to hold on, 'Tell me about the funeral you will arrange for me and what your own family tomb is like and where it is, and whether –' Mr Kan said, 'Please! Hurry! Tell me!'

'Who are they? Why is there nothing to be gained because of who they are?' Yin, his hand squeezing at the phone, bathed in sweat, pleaded desperately, 'Kan, tell me who they are! Tell me what they want! The things they take from the coffins – are they –' He hardly knew what to say, '*Are they parts of the bodies?*'

'Yes.' Kan said, 'My tomb – our shared tomb – what position does it have? Is it high, overlooking the sea, or mountains, or –' He asked, his voice going, 'Where is it?' Kan said without waiting for an answer, 'I went to see my own plot in Soong's because I was concerned – you must station guards about your own family tomb! I read once in a Western book that a hundred years ago when there were grave-robbers, families stationed armed guards and dogs about the graves of their loved ones – you must do something like that! You are a Western-educated man – you must do something like that to protect us all! We cannot enter heaven if our graves have been violated.' He began gasping, fighting for his breath. Kan said in a panic, 'They are coming. I see them. They are coming. We cannot win against them! They are not ordinary criminals, they are soldiers! They are not doing these things for any personal motive or gain – they are doing them because they have been ordered to!'

'*Run!*'

'If I run and you call the police it will do no good! They are soldiers! I know the look of them! If you kill them or catch them there will be thousands more to take their places!' Kan, shouting, said, 'No! No! Share my last few moments with me! We may have to spend eternity together in our tomb – let us at least talk together!' Kan said suddenly calmly, 'My life has been a long and uneventful one.' It was as if he put his mouth close to the receiver to nestle in to Yin, to shut out what, outside the booth was coming towards him. 'When young, in Shensi province, I had hoped to become a scholar, but the finances of my family did not permit it and I was at first apprenticed to a wood carver,' – he said with what sounded like a chuckle, 'I still smell sometimes the smell of wood shavings and of glue and the deep rosiness of fine camphor, but again, the apprenticeship was so long and my abilities and the abilities of my family to subsidize me so meagre that I –' He said, 'I am a very religious man. I have never married and I have no living relatives and I have always tried to obey the precepts of good and moral behaviour in both my private and business dealings.' He said quickly, 'I will hang up before they come. I want you to know that you will discover nothing in your researches about my life that will cause you to regret your decision to let me lie in your family tomb. I have done no great or small evil to any man since I became old and those that I did when I was young I have amply repaid and no man holds any grudge against me.' He said softly, 'Will you believe me?'

There was no point. Yin said softly, 'Yes, I believe you.'

'And your family, your family, I know, is an ancient and honourable one. If they were not, as a relatively young man, you would never have been entrusted with the position you hold in the Society. Your position speaks that, for generations, your family has been upright and respected and noble.' He asked, 'This is true?'

'Yes.'

'They were landowners or scholars or officials?'

Yin said quietly, 'The ancestral patriarch of my family was the cousin of the first Emperor of China, Ch'in Shih-huang-ti, two thousand years ago. The lineage is unbroken.'

There was a hush. Kan said in a whisper, 'Have I asked too much?'

He was weeping. He had wept at the names of the dead on the scrolls and he wept now. Yin said softly, 'No, you have not asked too much.'

'– that I –'

Yin said quietly, 'You and I will lie together in eternity. In Heaven my ancestral patriarch will make you his friend.' He heard a sound, a scrabbling, a thumping sound. Yin said, 'Kan! Kan! Are you there?' In his office, Yin shrieked down the line, '*KAN!!*' The line went dead. True to his word, at the last, he had hung up.

Yin screamed into the dead instrument in his hand, 'Kan! I lied! My family have always been nothing but money lenders and merchants! I lied to keep you talking!' He shrieked, '*KAN!*'

Ta chia tu shih ming, pan tien pu yu jên. 'Our destinies have been set with no reference to our wishes at all.' In the phone booth, looking directly into the officer's face, Mr Kan smiled. He looked down at the officer's hands and watched as, carefully, slowly, he removed the glove from his right hand and formed his fist with the second finger outermost like a spearhead.

Mr Kan said softly in Mandarin, 'Good iron does not make nails, nor a good man a soldier.' He wore his long silk gown and cap. He looked down at his uncut scholar's fingernail and smiled. Mr Kan said, 'My eternity is set. You hold no fear for me and I will tell you nothing.' He saw the officer draw back his fist and his eyes flicker to Kan's temple to the place where the death blow would go. Kan said quickly, 'Let me adjust my clothing.'

'*Kill him!*' It was another one of them. It was the driver from the Mercedes. The driver, running sweat, filthy from the grave in the cemetery, shouted in Mandarin, '*Kill him quickly and let us go!*'

He saw the officer's eyes. There was something there. Mr Kan said sadly, 'All this, is it so important that you must do things that are —' He saw the eyes change. He saw an order there. He was in the phone booth, unafraid, not leaning on any part of its construction, not taking any support or comfort from any part of its solidity. Mr Kan said, smiling, 'You —' Mr Kan said all at once, '*I will lie in eternity with Emperors!*' He saw the fist come back. He saw the strength in it. He saw the order. He saw the eyes.

He turned his head slightly to one side and the officer, driving hard for the temple, with no reluctance or lessening of the blow, the motion once started unstoppable, crushing bones, nerves and blood vessels with the single terrible blow, killed him instantly where he stood.

He wept. All his life, all his education, everything he had ever been or known or worked to learn, had counted for nothing, and, at the end, like the lowest of the low, like the poor he protected, like all the hopeless and unsuccessful and afraid of the world, he had, at the end, only barren grief.

In his office, John Yin, all that he was, putting his head on his hands on his desk, his body shaking convulsively, cried with no shame or solace, like a child.

10

The complainers were not complaining any more: they were beginning to form a lynch mob. At the corner of Jade Street, Auden, glancing back to where the Polynesian, the Melanesian and the dead-letter man flitted through the crowds spying on him, said to the lunatic sitting in the gutter sucking postcards, 'Deliver the mail!' He saw the dead-letter man see him see him and duck into a doorway. They were all against him. It wasn't his fault their mail wasn't getting through. It was Spencer's. Auden, taking Spencer by the scruff of the neck and, in case any more little schoolgirls were around, giving him a pat before he clamped his fingers around the carotid artery, ordered him with a fixed grin, 'Please deliver the mail, Bill.'

Spencer said, 'Erk.'

Auden gave his throat another twist.

Spencer said, 'Erk! Erk!'

There weren't any more little schoolgirls around. They were all at school. Auden shouted down, *'Deliver the mail!'* As well as people out to spy on him there were people out to blow him up. He didn't need any more people. Auden, still grinning, showing by the moment more and more teeth, said in final warning, 'If you don't get up on to your feet and start behaving like a normal person I'm going to drag you up by your bloody ears, haul you into the middle of the road and throw you under the nearest bloody padded van!' He saw Spencer turn his head to look up at him. His face looked a little black. Auden said,

'You're not getting the gun back!' Auden said, 'Stop sucking that postcard!' He saw for an instant the name and address on the back of the card. The name was John Kamehameha. Auden said in horror, 'That's his postcard! That's the postcard the bloody Hawaiian or whatever he was threatened to kill me over!' He reached down to get it. Spencer pulled away. The Hawaiian was about six foot five. He was down the street watching with his mate the Melanesian. Auden said, 'You stole his bloody postcard!'

'No.' He spoke. Spencer, shaking his head, took another postcard from his bag and then another. Spencer, holding them up, said, gasping, 'No, I stole this one from the dead-letter man.' He took one of the other postcards and sucked it. Spencer said, 'They're all for John Kamehameha.' He turned them over in his hand. 'They're all postcards of the sands of Waikiki.' He tried to twist out of Auden's grasp. Auden was looking down at the postcards and had forgotten about Spencer's artery. Spencer said in a gasp, 'They've all had the addresses changed with an eraser so that they're undeliverable.' The postcard he had taken from the dead-letter man's office had UNDELIVERABLE. RETURN TO DEAD LETTER OFFICE HONOLULU written across it. Spencer said, 'Suck it.'

Auden said, 'No.'

Spencer, patting the gutter beside him, said invitingly, 'Sit down, Phil.' He took the undeliverable card and sucked it. Spencer said, 'Time to go through your bag for postcards.' He said encouragingly, 'I've been thinking about it. I've worked it out.' He saw Auden glance quickly over his shoulder. Spencer said, 'No one's throwing anything in the bags to set them on fire because whatever's setting them on fire is already inside the bag.' He reached into his own bag and took out a pile of letters held together by a rubber band. Spencer said, 'The postcards with the changed addresses have to sit next to letters in the bag with approximately the same street address and number.' He began to go through the letters. He was about to suck them.

Auden said, 'We X-rayed all the letters.'

'And saw what?'

Auden said, 'Nothing.'

Spencer said, 'Here, sit down beside me on the kerb.'

Auden said, 'No.'

Spencer said, '*See?*'

He saw the multinational posse no doubt making notes on him for the official chucking-out-of-the-public-service tribunal that would send him back to a beat counting the cow pats on the Norfolk Broads. Auden said lamely, 'You promised if I let you come you wouldn't talk.'

'Right.' He shut up. He sat on the kerb sucking his postcards and staring off into space.

Auden said, 'What postcards? They're just postcards of the bloody sand in Hawaii.' Everyone down the road seemed to have disappeared. Auden said, 'What do you mean all the addresses have been changed?'

Spencer said, 'Can I talk?'

Auden made a growling noise. Anything was better than the fire bucket.

Spencer said, 'They've all been changed by the same hand.' He held up the postcard he had been sucking. It was soggy. Spencer said, 'And the hand that changed the address so it would be undeliverable is the same hand that wrote across it UNDELIVERABLE. RETURN TO DEAD LETTER OFFICE HONOLULU.' Spencer said, 'The dead-letter man wrote it.' He looked down the road, but the dead-letter man was nowhere to be seen. Spencer said thoughtfully, 'Now, carefully, think through all the possibilities. What would *you* think that might mean?'

Oh, no . . . He had done it. He had finally done it. Yellow T-shirts in banana shops, American tourists with accents, rubber noses, funny wigs, turbans, beards, Europeans down on their luck, Quasimodo limps, Portuguese – and now, at last, he had finally done it. He had entered the perfect, ultimate disguise. He was disguised in some sort of ultimate, final nod to masquerade in the disguise of the Great Disguise Artist himself. He was Sherlock bloody Holmes – in disguise as a disguised European detective in Hong Kong sitting at the junction of Jade Street sucking postcards. Auden said sadly, 'Oh, no . . .' Down the street, flitting from shopway to shopway, he even had his collection of Polynesians, Melanesians and inscrutable lethal Orientals. All he needed now was a Dyak with a blowgun. Auden, wishing someone might come along and obligingly set fire to his bag and put him out of his misery, said in heartfelt tragedy, 'Oh, no . . . !' It had never happened to Gary Cooper. Auden said, 'Oh, no, no, no, *no*!'

Spencer, smiling at him happily and offering up the undeliverable stolen postcard, said with a warm nod, 'Here, suck it.' He raised his finger to make himself crystal clear above the sounds inside his head of the hansoms and landaus clip-clopping their way along Baker Street outside 221B (or maybe it was above the violin music in his head). Spencer said, 'Tell me what you make of that taste.' He said before Auden could speak (no doubt he was the author of the standard monograph on the tastes of Waikiki sands postcards), 'Quick, tell me what you think it is!'

Auden said, 'It's sand.'

Holmes said, 'Ha, ha!'

Auden said, 'It's a cheap postcard from Hawaii with a bit of yellow sand stuck on it.' He wanted to sit down on the kerb and cry. He wasn't going to sit down on the kerb. 'It's like a Christmas card with a bit of glitter stuck on it to look like snow.' Auden said – Auden said, 'Why the hell am I even having this conversation with you?' Auden said, at the end, 'Bill, I've just about –'

'*That's what they want us to think!*' Spencer, getting up and thrusting the card under Auden's, nose said, 'Here! Taste it!'

Auden said, 'It's sand.' He sniffed it.

'Don't sniff it! Taste it!'

Auden, flicking his tongue across the corner of the card, said, 'It's sand! It's sand! OK? It's bloody *sand*!'

'And this?' He produced another card. How many cards did he have? Spencer said, 'What about this?'

'It's sand too!' The dead-letter man was following them not because people were blowing up his mailmen's bags or because people were even blowing up his mailmen but because the mail was being sucked to death. Auden said, 'All the poor bugger did was return the postcard to the place from whence (his mind was going – *whence?*) from whence it came!' He looked at Holmes and felt sorry for Moriarty.

Spencer said, 'Those two postcards you just sucked are the two from my bag that have had the addresses changed.' He produced again, as from nowhere, the card he had stolen from the dead-letter man's office and held it to Auden's face with the UNDELIVERABLE legend across it. Spencer said, 'Now suck this one.'

Auden said, 'It's sand.' If he had not had to borrow Spencer's gun none of this would have happened. Borrowing put you under an obligation. It was like copping a ride with a lunatic. Until he got you to where you were going you had to be nice to him. Auden said without looking at it, 'It's sand.'

'No.' Spencer, shaking his head, said quietly, 'No, it isn't. It might have been when it came into the post office, and it might have been when you carried it about, and it might have been before the dead-letter man wrote across it that it was to be sent back to Hawaii, but it isn't now.'

'*What the hell is it now then* – dog bloody turds?'

'No.' Spencer smiled. He patted Auden gently on the arm. 'No.' He said gently, 'Here, try it. Have a little taste.' He glanced back down the road to see the dead-letter man disappear quickly into a doorway. Spencer said quietly, 'No, what it is now, is *heroin*.' He was staring happily away into the distance – with all the heroin he had sucked it was a miracle he wasn't part of that distance. He saw Auden's face. Poor, good, dumb John Watson.

Spencer, knowing all, scratching gently at the side of his neck in an old Himalayan restorative scratch the monks of Nepal had taught him once in The Case of Queen Victoria's Nepalese Diadem (never recorded), asked with his eyes glittering, 'Well, old friend, just what do you make of that?' He said softly, 'Erk?' He said softly, happy, 'Hmm?'

He said in triumph, 'Erk! Erk! *Erk!*'

'George . . . ? . . . Ian?'

The voice said, 'Hal.' The voice said, 'Who's that?'

O'Yee said, 'Harrington.'

'Ah.' The voice said, 'Yes, Harrington, quickly make your report.'

Harrington of the Secret Service said quickly, 'Listen, I

know it's stupid to ring on an open line, but this is so urgent it can't wait.' He waited. They were listening. O'Yee said, 'You know the Hong Kong Station of the Ministry Of External Calm has moved –' He paused. They did know. O'Yee said, 'There's a raid planned on the new address by the civil police in connection with another matter and you'd better get our surveillance people away or stop the raid before it happens.' He said darkly, 'Or *the other matter* could be compromised.'

'Hmm.' The voice said, 'Hmm, the other matter.' The voice said, 'Good security, Harrington.'

O'Yee said, 'I do my best.'

'Which station is running the police raid?'

O'Yee said, 'Yellowthread Street. But don't worry, we've got a good man there.'

The voice said, 'Who?'

O'Yee said, 'Detective Senior Inspector O'Yee.' He said in a whisper, 'Just give O'Yee the address you don't want his people to hit and O'Yee will make sure his people don't hit it.'

'Right.' The voice said, 'What's he like?'

'O'Yee?'

'Yes.'

Well, what could he say? O'Yee said admiringly, 'Well . . .' He wanted that address. O'Yee said, 'Oh, you know . . .' O'Yee said in a whisper, 'Bloody *brilliant!*'

There was a silence. They were writing it down.

O'Yee said, 'OK?'

'Thanks, Harrington.' The voice said in a whisper, '*Excalibur!*'

He hung up.

In the public booth of the Hong Bay Telephone Company in Wyang Street, the Captain dialled the number again and waited.

There was no reply. The number merely rang and rang and rang and no one picked up the receiver.

The Resurrection Squad was posted in and around the building to give him security. The last one had unnerved them a little. He knew they all had their hands close to their guns.

The Captain, rubbing at the second joint of the second finger of his right hand where he had killed the old man, stopped to think for a moment.

He had his orders.

He dialled the number again and waited.

The number rang and rang and rang.

It was an assignment like any other. He knew all the procedures. He was a professional. He remained calm.

Glancing at his watch, he decided to stay in the booth for another five minutes exactly and then try the number again.

There was a faint bruise forming on his joint and he flexed it to keep it supple.

Five minutes exactly and no more.

He glanced at his watch and waited.

Down the private road from the cemetery, PCs Lee and Cho had charge of the examination of Kan. There was only a small, dead old man lying doubled up in a telephone booth to examine: there was not much. In the servants' section of the cemetery there was the awful, twisted body of a creature who had been in the ground for five months and was no longer human. There was the corpse of a man with both arms missing in a broken-open coffin. Standing over the hole, watching as Doctor Macarthur, oblivious of the horror, leant full length over the awful thing half covered by its linen winding sheet, Feiffer said for the second time to John Yin, 'Are you absolutely sure he said they were soldiers?'

'Yes.' The smell from the open grave was awful. He saw Macarthur look up and read on his face only fascination. John Yin, unnerved, forming his hands into fists, said, 'Yes. He told me they were soldiers.'

'What sort of soldiers?'

'They looked like soldiers. They stood like soldiers.' Yin, shaking his head, willing Macarthur to get out of there and close the lid on the thing inside that had once been a man, said, 'I don't know!'

'Had Kan been a soldier himself? Would he have known? Or did he just mean –'

'He didn't say they were in uniform.' There was a mound of earth where they had dug down to the coffin and splintered wood where they had crowbarred it open. 'Of course they weren't in uniform!' Yin, a tic starting on his face, said suddenly in English, 'What the hell do you think they were? The goddamned West Point guard of honour in goddamned white ducks and shakos? He said they stood like soldiers!' He said angrily to Macarthur, 'You! How did he die – Kan? What killed him?' He saw Macarthur glance to Feiffer. Yin said, 'A single blow delivered to the side of the head, right? A god-damned silent-killing blow or whatever they call it!'

Feiffer said, 'It's a Special Forces method of killing.' So was the pressure on the windpipe expertly applied that had killed Mrs Ping in China. Feiffer, laying his hand gently on Yin's arm as Macarthur reached down to turn the creature in the coffin out of its winding sheet and hold the sheet up to the light, said quietly, 'John, if he didn't tell you anything, then . . .'

'He told me he wanted to rest through eternity without his body being desecrated!' He saw Macarthur free the corpse in the coffin and he saw what it looked like. Yin said, 'For Christ's sake – can't you just cover him up again and leave him?' It was a game. It was some sort of awful, horrible, ghastly treasure hunt game – for everyone. They had glanced at Kan cursorily and left him in the charge of the uniformed cops and the fingerprint men and then – all of them – had run slathering with curiosity and interest up to the graveyard to see what fascinating, marvellous, interesting, great stories for the memoirs of my life in the exotic East the Resurrection Squad had given them this time. Yin, at the end of his control, said, 'Why can't you all just go away and leave us all *alone*!' He heard Macarthur, totally oblivious to anything, say quickly, 'Harry!' and hold up part of the winding sheet for Feiffer's inspection. Yin, closing his eyes, said to no one, to anyone who might listen – to no one who did – 'Please . . . please, just leave us all alone . . .'

'Harry, look!' He had the winding sheet up in his hands like a magician with his silk cloth. Macarthur, turning it first one way and then the other, said quickly, 'Look, look at the colour of the material: the decomposition stains and here –' He lifted up one corner – 'Look at the marks the earth falling in from the open grave has left. Look at the colour. It's leached topsoil and shallow clay.' He pulled the sheet down and with a flick laid it in the coffin by the twisted leathery feet to set off something. 'And look at that: it's dark, deep, dried-out soil and deep-clay strata.' He said to Yin's face, unable to read the expressions of the living, 'I'm a bit of an amateur gardener in my own small way. It's not local soil.'

'John . . .' Feiffer, his hand still on Yin's arm, said quietly, 'You go home now.' He looked down at Macarthur and shook his head to silence him. Feiffer said, 'If there's anything we want you for –' He saw Yin's face. Feiffer said encouragingly, 'There must be arrangements about – about Kan –'

Macarthur said in triumph from the grave, 'This isn't the first time this corpse has been buried!' He wondered why the hell no one was listening. Macarthur, not to be denied, climbing out of the grave with a handful of desiccated soil in his hand, thrusting it under Yin's and Feiffer's noses, said angrily, 'Look! Look! This corpse, at one stage, was buried at least twenty or thirty feet in open ground without a coffin!' He couldn't be sure until he got Scientific to do a full analysis. Macarthur said, 'Isn't anybody even interested?' Both arms had been taken. The thing in the smashed open coffin looked like a blackened doll a child had torn apart in a tantrum of anger.

Macarthur, briefly chasing after Feiffer and Yin as Feiffer led the man towards the cemetery gate, said in total, utter amazement, 'Look! Doesn't anyone even want to *look*?'

There was no reply. At the other end of the line the phone rang and rang and rang and there was no reply. *Win Kai Sun*. They had known when they broke open the coffin that the man inside had been burned to death with petrol. It had unnerved them, that, and later the old man in the telephone booth.

In the public telephone area of the Hong Bay Telephone Company on Wyang Street the Captain, still rubbing at the joint of his finger, put down the receiver. The man he had waited to speak to on the phone called himself a Colonel.

It was not a rank the Captain cared to or would acknowledge.

He looked at his watch. His squad was well trained and in

position and, if they were growing increasingly nervous, they would not let it show.

One more time.

Rubbing at his finger, putting coins into the telephone, carefully, he began dialling the number he had been given as his one and only contact with a man whose face he had never seen.

She saw him. For an instant, in a black station wagon in Icehouse Street, Miss Fan saw him. *It was him!* He was driving fast, trying to get somewhere in a hurry as if he was late for an appointment. It was him.

It was him!

She began running, looking for a taxi, but there was none around. It was him. He was heading north. She called, because there was nothing else she could do, '*Kau!* Colonel *Kau!*' but he was gone in the traffic around the corner into Yellowthread Street and away and it had only been the wildest coincidence that she had seen him at all.

Find me . . .

She would.

She would find him.

On the street, oblivious to the people passing on either side of her, she stood staring up the street at the traffic and thinking about the pistol in her bag.

It was time.

She went to find a phone to ring O'Yee.

There was one other thing. Standing in the grave, straddling the coffin, looking down with a smile playing about his face, Macarthur waited. There was one other thing. He had the handful of soil in a little glassine envelope in his pocket and, patting it, staring down at the lined base of the coffin and the seals and broken wires on either side of it, Macarthur waited, humming.

Soldiers. The Chinese funeral director or whatever he was had said they were soldiers. That figured. Along the lining of the coffin where the left arm had been he could see an indentation, a stain where, for a long time – for at least the five

months the corpse had been in the ground *the second time* –
something had lain alongside him, gripped hard in his hand.

He heard Feiffer coming back: he heard his footfalls on the
hard, leached ground.

He waited, looking down at the indentation and the stain.
Macarthur, still humming, looked up to see Feiffer come. He
said softly, before the man could hear, 'Harry . . . look.' He
was sorry if he had said something wrong. It didn't matter.
Macarthur, grinning, said, 'Look! Look what the dead man in
here was carrying!' He gave Feiffer no chance at all to say
anything. Macarthur said, 'Look! Look at the outline!' He said
in triumph, '*Look!*'

It was something a servant burned to death in China, who
had been buried once before, had been carrying in his hand. It
was what, along with the other arm, the soldiers had taken.

It was clear, as clear as the colour of the earlier earth caught
up in the coffin and the winding sheet. It was there, outlined,
picked up on the lining by oxidization and stain and decomposition. It was clear. Macarthur said, 'Look! Look at the
marks and lines and indentations! Look!'

It was a shadow.

He heard Feiffer say softly, 'God Almighty . . . !'

It was the shadow of a sword.

11

Old Holmes might have done the standard monograph on Waikiki sand, but what he knew about Sharps' buffalo guns with self-contained paper cartridges you could have put in his cocaine needle and still have room left over for the cocaine.

Particularly since, of recent date, Holmes had given up shooting cocaine and taken up sucking heroin.

In the doorway of the four-storey apartment building in Jade Street he was sitting sucking, falling over backwards. Auden, shaking him, said, 'Don't suck! Smell!'

Spencer said, 'No.' He grinned. His eyes were turning into saucers. Spencer said, 'The postcards are from Hawaii to someone called John Kamehameha . . .' He grinned. He asked, 'Is this where he lives?'

Auden said, 'Yes!' He thrust a letter under Spencer's nose. Auden said, 'Smell it!'

Spencer said happily, 'Sure.' He didn't. Spencer said, 'And what happens is that the dead-letter man sneaks into the sorting office and changes the street number on the address so the cards are undeliverable. Then, when they come back to him undelivered, he takes the sand off' – he said, blearily, happily, 'I wonder how he does that . . . And then he recoats the beach scene on the postcard with pure H, dyed yellow –' He said as if it was part of the earlier thought (he looked blank: he had forgotten the earlier thought), 'I wonder how he does that? And then he sends it back to the dead-letter office in Honolulu, and because there's never a return address on a postcard it gets put to one side and –' He said, 'I wonder who picks it up? The Honolulu dead-letter office man or a cleaner or what . . . ? And that way he's got a perfect method of smuggling pure H into the United States without anyone noticing a thing.' He said, 'Hmm.' He had done all the brainwork. He closed his eyes to fall over backwards and go to sleep.

Auden, shaking him, said, 'You're bloody *zonked*!' Auden, pushing and shoving at him and finding his shoulder pure jello, said in disgust, 'That doesn't explain why the bags keep blowing up!' He had the Sharps' buffalo gun theory worked out to a T. Auden, thrusting a letter under Spencer's nose, said, 'Look! This is a letter that was next to the postcard in the bag! It's got the same address, one number out – for the next apartment block!' He ordered the dope fiend, 'Smell it!'

The dope fiend had another suck on the postcard. The dope fiend said, smiling, 'Nitrated paper.' He drifted off to sleep.

Auden said, 'No, it's nitrated paper! It's the same sort of paper buffalo hunters used in their Sharps' buffalo guns! It's impregnated with – with –' He didn't know what it was impregnated with.

Spencer said, 'Potassium chlorate.' He sniffed. He said, nodding, 'Yep, that's what it is. If you even look at it with a match it self-destructs.' He was an expert. He was doing the same thing: self-destructing. Spencer said, 'Well, that's it. The sand on the postcard rubs against the letter in the bag and makes it catch fire.' He said, 'So all we have to do is set up a stake-out at the Honolulu dead-letter office when the next postcard gets returned and see who picks it up and then we can –' His eyes glazed. He was falling backwards. His head looked as if, any moment, it was going to fall off his neck and he wouldn't mind. Spencer, grinning, said happily, '*Book him, Dano!*'

Auden said in an even tone, 'I hate you.'

Spencer said, 'It's the stamp. I told you it was the stamp. The secret lies in the stamp.' He had worked it all out. Spencer, patting Auden gently on the shoulder, said, 'Hold up the nitrated letter to the light and you can see that behind the flap there's something else – just the faintest shadow. That's a little coating of phosphorus: that's what sets the nitrated paper off – it's an anti-interference device of the simplest kind.' He said, 'Ho, ho, ho.' He wished he had his old Persian slipper full of shag tobacco. 'That's what actually destroys the letter so no one can get at it and find out what's inside.' Or his violin. He had always wanted to play the violin. Spencer said, 'It didn't show up on the X-rays because of what's inside.'

Watson, getting a wee bit weary of chronicling Holmes' adventures in which he always came out as the bumbling shit, said in a snarl, 'OK, so what is inside?' He held it up to the light. There was nothing inside. The stamp was a multi-coloured New Guinea airmail postage. Auden said, 'Well? Well?'

The Great Mind said, 'Hmm.' The famous hawk-nosed profile glanced down at the sidewalk and began tracing little patterns on it with his finger. The Great Disguise Artist said, 'Ha, ha, ha . . .' He said, recreating one of his celebrated roles, 'Erk.' He scratched his head. He looked vaguely down the street and saw the dead-letter man, John Kamehameha – it had to be him, he was the only Hawaiian on the block – and a Melanesian built like a brick who got nitrated letters sent to him, bearing down on him in a posse. He shrugged (he merely put it down to hallucination) and said without the faintest idea in the world, 'Gee, Phil, I haven't got the foggiest.'

He did. Auden said, 'I do!' (He didn't see anyone bearing down on him.) Auden said, '*Butterflies!* The one thing you smuggle in from New Guinea that's worth a fortune overseas.' He wasn't stupid. He could hold a letter up to the light the other way and fool old Holmes every time. Auden said, 'Non-X-rayable, illegal, protected as an endangered species New Guinea *butterflies!*' He could also read addresses. The letter was addressed to the butterfly man in the corridor. Auden said, at last, finally – the *mot juste* that sent old Holmes into retirement beekeeping in Dorset or Sussex or wherever the hell it was – 'Butterflies! We've got two separate smuggling cases here and I've cracked them both!' He said, shoving the letters and postcards back into his bag a moment before the multi-national lynch-mob all reached him at once, 'Butterflies! And they're being smuggled in in nitrate-paper envelopes so no one

can open them and find out what they are and they're being –'
He said, 'Oh my God!' He saw the dead-letter man and the
Polynesian and the Melanesian all in mid-air, about to leap on
him in concert and he began to run into the corridor, drawing
his gun. Auden, turning, yanking at the weapon from a back
pocket that might have been designed for a lot of things but not
gun-yanking, shouted in warning, 'Bill! Bill! Look out!' He
heard the Hawaiian as he leapt over Spencer in the doorway,
shriek, 'Where are all the postcards from my family?' He heard
the Melanesian shout, 'My letters! Someone keeps burning all
my valuable, irreplaceable collectors' letters!' He heard the
dead-letter man, Communist bastard that he was, shriek in
Cantonese, *'Kill!'*

He saw them all stop and look at each other in surprise. He
saw – He saw Spencer turn and grin.

Auden yelled, *'Spencer!'*

He tried to get the gun out. At last, he was going to get the
opportunity to shoot something. He saw Spencer start to rise
and, zonked, grinning happily, raise his postbag to crack the
nearest shrieker over the head. The gun came out. He saw the
muzzle go down range and for the merest, happiest, most
joyful moment, actually centre itself on Spencer's grinning
mug. He saw everyone freeze. Auden said, 'OK, you can relax!
It's all over!' He saw the Melanesian butterfly smuggler tense
to spring. Nobody tensed to spring when Gary Cooper was
around. Auden said, 'OK, you people are all under –' He heard
a fizz. Auden said sadly, 'Oh, no . . .'

He had put the postcard and the letter back in his bag. It
proved it. Oh, Watson . . . Oh, shit.

Auden said sadly, watching as Spencer began walking slowly, carefully around the arrested men for the fire bucket,
'Oh . . .'

Gary Cooper never cried.

Auden said softly, 'Oh, Spencer! Oh . . . *God*!!'

He stood waiting, obligingly, beaten, defeated, just not one
of his good days, until, a few seconds later, right on cue, his bag
blew up.

*

In the public telephone booths in the Hong Bay Telephone Company office on Wyang Street Miss Fan dialled the number for the Detectives' Room at the Yellowthread Street Police Station and waited for someone to pick up the line.

She heard his voice. O'Yee said briskly, 'Detective Senior Inspector O'Yee.'

She had a quote from Thoreau ready. The quote was from Thoreau's essay on civil disobedience. The quote was, *Come boys, it is now time to lock up*.

'Detective Senior Inspector O'Yee —'

She tapped at the little table in the booth with her fingers.

'*Hullo!*'

Her bag was unzipped. It was a coincidence seeing Kau, but she had not been ready. She drummed her fingers hard on the table in the booth.

'*Is there anyone there?*'

It was not time. It was coming, but it was not time yet. She could not decide.

Unsure, glancing down at the open bag and the pistol it contained, shaking her head, she hung up.

In the Mercedes, the Captain, with his squad sitting around him, took out his envelope of sealed orders and ripping it open carefully from the side, took out the single sheet of paper it contained.

The paper had written on it in block Chinese characters an address and, below it, because none of the squad had ever been in Hong Kong before or knew its streets, the same address written in English.

It was over, finished. All the time had run out.

The Captain said quietly to his squad in Mandarin, 'No more graves.' At his feet there were the shovels and picks they had used covered in hessian sacking. He could smell the smell of death and decay on them. The Captain said encouragingly, 'We'll find somewhere near the harbour and clean the car out.'

In the trunk of the car they had their Ingram machine pistols carefully packed in oiled paper. The Captain said quietly, 'No more graves.'

Even in the air-conditioned car he was hot. He touched at the perspiration on his brow.

The Captain said, 'First the harbour, then tonight, we can finish.'

He thought it had been a fully successful operation.

He still needed them sharp, but as someone who had led them for a very long time, he knew that they at least needed the thought of a respite.

The Captain, permitting himself one of his rare smiles, said to hearten them, 'By tonight we should be on a plane for home.'

As a touchstone, he was watching the driver's shoulders.

He saw them sag in relief.

If they were soldiers and it was some sort of military operation then it was one that had gone wrong from the outset. It was happening too quickly to be going right. It had happened too quickly from the moment Hwa's headless body had been dragged from the harbour – they – whoever they were – had panicked and begun tearing the coffins out of the ground at a pace that could not be controlled or covered, and it had brought them to Soong's private cemetery by day and it had brought Mr Kan to a sudden death in a phone box. *Some of the bodies had been in the ground for over two years. There had been plenty of time to plan patiently and execute their removal by stealth*. Instead, it was all happening at once.

Armies – soldiers – young men under orders from older, more conservative men, did not act like young men and rip coffins apart and sink them in harbours or crowbar open graves and leave the bodies of witnesses around: they proceeded carefully, one stage at a time, until their object was achieved. They were human, prone to fatigue and loss of morale and slip-ups: older, wiser men knew that. It was only in bad war movies or on television that the John Waynes of this world fought tirelessly, went from one horror to another, and still succeeded. If Kan had been right and they were soldiers – and Chinese soldiers at that – they could not live out the last two days and the sights they had seen and still be expected to be fresh, alert and in grasp of their original plan.

Their original plan had gone wrong. Or, if it had not, it had been speeded up by some outside source, from Canton – from something that, like Kan, had happened unexpectedly and changed everything.

What it had been had been the killing or the suicide of the mortuary attendant in the Canton Military Hospital. It had to have been. At the graveside, Feiffer, gazing down at the burned corpse, asked Macarthur, 'Anything else?'

Macarthur was back in the coffin, rummaging gently through the coloured earths and collecting them into glassine packets for analysis. He shook his head.

Over almost three years – more – it had all been planned, all the bodies chosen, selected, at least one of the deaths created especially for the task, and then, suddenly, with the first body weighed down and sunk in the harbour – sooner or later *discoverable* – the whole thing had taken on a life of its own.

The seals on all the coffins had been genuine, or if they were not (and he had the word of Owens the Trustworthy for that) they would have required the facilities of an institution at least as vast as the Royal Mint to forge.

In China they had facilities like that.

In China they would not have faked a suicide using an old gun and new cartridges and left the body by a railway spur at a hospital where whatever they were doing was taking place.

In China, the poor and the powerless from Hong Kong were being murdered to fill coffins filled with something else.

In China, if there was something the size of a coffin to fill (with what? Heroin? Jade? Gold?) they would have simply filled a packing case, labelled it with diplomatic *laissez-passers* and sent it to one of their Embassies in another country and had another, friendly, neutral Embassy send it through to Hong Kong.

In China, they had negotiated the final return of Hong Kong, and all they had to do if they wanted to send something in was wait a few years and Customs would not have queried whatever it was they were sending in because they would have been controlling Customs themselves.

No, if it came from China, it was a private operation.

There were no private operations in China, and, if there were, they did not control military hospitals, mortuary attendants, the facilities to forge seals, or have unlimited travel permits to kill people all over China and see their papers and know that the people they killed were the right people whose coffins would not be opened to be reinterred in Hong Kong.

There was no one like that in China, no one who had that power.

Or was there? Was there someone like that? One man?

Was there anything that any one man could put in the coffins that would make that sort of risk worth it?

Human parts had gone into the coffins, *human parts*. Parts of human beings . . . At the grave, Feiffer, staring into the abyss, said softly, 'It's insane.' He saw Macarthur look up with the envelopes of earth in his hand. They were of different colours: the burned, ruined body, once had been buried in the earth before.

It was insane.

What the hell did they have when they put it all together?

They had nothing.

They had some sort of ghastly, rotting, vile collection of meat and stinking flesh. In at least one of the cases all they had were bones.

It was not heroin. It was not gold or jade or jewels or something from some B-grade movie writer's imagination – the solid jade Kwan Yin goddess of mercy or whatever was the favourite McGuffin at the moment because there was nothing in the world worth that much – what it was was the worst thing the Chinese mind could imagine: the dismemberment of the human body, the mixing of human bodies, and whatever the reason for it, if it was happening in China – if someone there was doing it, was planning it, then it was so awesome, so important, so desirable, that a squad of Chinese soldiers under orders from men of intellect and conservatism – from their political leaders – were prepared to risk everything, even failure, to get it.

There was nothing in the world like that.

It was political. It had to be political. It was happening at exactly the moment the political future of Hong Kong was being decided and there could be no other explanation.

If it was political and it affected the future of Hong Kong and China, all the Chinese had to do was wait a few years and none of it would have mattered.

It didn't matter now. No one would have dared embarrass them. No one was allowed to even ring them. Feiffer said suddenly, aloud, 'For God's sake, it's insane! All the Chinese have ever had to do in Hong Kong is march in! No one would have opposed them!' Feiffer said with sudden anger, 'What the hell was in there?'

What had been in there had been a human being who once had had a face and expectations.

What was in there now was a burned, blackened, rotting half-recognizable thing whose hope for immortality was gone.

What was in there was one of the poor and alone of the world, John Yin's poor and alone, the poor and alone of the oldest funeral society in the world. He glanced in at the box and saw the outline of the sword on the linen.

Even the Communists had never dared interfere with the burial practices of their people. They were pragmatists – they knew that even their system in the long view of history was as nothing and that the only eternals were death and proper burial. They knew that. That would never change. John Yin, the Harvard educated man of the world, the entrepreneur, the faultless English-speaker: he knew that. Feiffer said softly, 'I don't know what to do.' He thought of PC Lee. He saw Macarthur look up. Feiffer said in a whisper, 'I don't know what to do at all.'

All around him on the hills of the private cemetery were the things of timelessness, of Chinese eternity, of the lives and deaths and beliefs of the oldest civilized race on Earth – willow trees, streams with little cobbled paths running by them, tombs of marble and slate, little pagodas and, everywhere, in effigy and statue, the myriad gods and spirit-frighteners of a culture, like the ancient Egyptians, obsessed with a better, paradisical life not in this world but the next.

Death was so important, so inviolate, that Kan had not even had a door in his coffin repository, but put his faith in doorsteps and winding paths to frighten off the evil spirits.

He looked at the willow trees, at the symbols of longevity and peace, at the marble and the pagodas and the little effigies and at the place where the great tombs on the hill were. They were all not of this moment, but of the great moment, not of life and soldiers and days, but of eternity and the procession of generations and symbols, of the –

Feiffer said suddenly, 'Oh my God!'

There was nothing that would have justified what had happened.

There was one thing that would have justified what had happened.

He was afraid to look. With his eyes still on the trees and the emblems, Feiffer said to Macarthur, without looking at him, 'Turn back the linen – open it out.'

It was a shadow.

He heard the material rustle as Macarthur did as he was asked. He heard him clamber out of the grave.

It was the shadow of a sword.

He was afraid to look.

Macarthur said curiously, 'Harry? What is it?'

It was a shadow. It was outlined clearly on the linen where the decomposition and the gases had etched it as surely as if someone had drawn a line around it.

It was longer, figured. It was not a sword at all. It was more, when you knew what it was you were looking at, it was more like a long, ornate baton.

It was neither of those things.

It was, clearly outlined, figured, here and there, blurred and darkened from the long, ornate dragon that had encircled it, something else. It, too, like all the things in the cemetery, like all the things of eternity and timelessness, the things of importance, it too was a symbol, an emblem.

Feiffer, gazing at it, feeling his legs begin shaking with the realization, said in a whisper, 'God Almighty, I know what it is . . .'

It was a long sceptre.

*

'He was getting butterfly wings on the endangered species list posted in from New Guinea and he was sticking them onto the bodies of ordinary, boring butterflies he got here in Hong Kong. The wings came in in nitrated envelopes with a little bit of phosphorus stuck along the flap so that if anyone tried to open them they'd catch fire and destroy the evidence.' Auden, soaking wet, tapping the handcuffed Melanesian harder on the head than he needed to make his point, said to PC Yan in triumph, 'A clever ruse, but not one that could fool the man who knew anything about buffalo guns and nitrate-paper cartridges.' He saw PC Yan was not one of those who knew about buffalo guns and nitrate-paper cartridges. Auden, lowering the level of the conversation to something he could understand said, 'The dead-letter man here —' He was also squatting, handcuffed. He also got a bang on the head. 'He was re-routing sand-covered postcards from Hawaii so they were undeliverable and then re-coating them with pure heroin and sending them back to his contact who works in the dead-letter office in Honolulu for distribution into the US.' The Hawaiian was a poor innocent postcard receiver whose only crime was assault and battery on the police. He was not squatting. He was not handcuffed. He was about six foot five tall. He did not get a bang on the head. Auden said magnanimously, 'We've decided to let him off.'

The Hawaiian reached for his postcards. Auden pulled them away. Auden said, 'Evidence.' The Hawaiian said, 'Grr.'

PC Yan said, impressed, 'It must have been a monumental battle, Mr Auden.' There were squatting bodies, black eyes, soaked mailmen, burned mail-bags and, for good measure, a heroin-laden dope-fiend down-on-his-luck European snoring away happily in a corner.

Auden said, 'Yes, it was.'

PC Yan said, 'That's a clever disguise, sir.' He looked at the remnants of Auden's turban and beard. Yan said obsequiously, 'It suits you.' He looked down at Spencer. Spencer, like Coleridge, was content to eat lotuses. Yan said, 'Should I call an ambulance or just leave him here?'

The Hawaiian said, 'Give me my goddamned postcards! They're from my goddamned family in Honolulu! They never write me letters! They just send me postcards asking for money!' He said, 'Give me my goddamned postcards! They come every day! That's the only way I even know my goddamned family is still alive!' He made a grab for them, 'Give them to me or I'll –' He picked up the fire bucket and refilled it from the tap. The Hawaiian, advancing on Auden, said warningly, 'Give me my goddamned postcards!'

His last case. Holmes, the sound of a bugle blowing far off penetrating to that part of him that never slept, said, rising to his feet, 'Now, look, it is my opinion that . . .' He saw the bucket of water come swishing in his direction.

Spencer, awaking, said, 'Phil –!'

He saw Auden catch the full force of it.

He saw, for an instant, the ordinary US stamp on the postcard peel back and show just the corner of –

The Great Detective said, 'Ah, the two cents Hawaiian missionary of 1851.' It was unsmudged. Spencer said in amazement, 'Unsmudged with ink – an unused example!' He looked at Auden. Auden looked back at him. Spencer said, 'Ah.'

Spencer's eyes were as wide as saucers. He was zonked. Outside, as the paddy wagon arrived, he heard, for the briefest of brief moments, the sound of hansom cab wheels on cobbled streets. Inside his head it was forever 1887. Poor old Watson. He was dripping.

Spencer, rising to his feet, looking around for his ultimate disguise: his deerstalker and pipe, said happily, having waited all his life to say it, 'Watson, my dear old friend, but it was all – all just so *elementary*!'

He smiled.

He had one last disguise.

He produced it.

It was the disguise of a man about to be hit in the mouth.

As usual, it was perfect.

Mind you, in Watson, he had the perfect assistant.

The blow was so hard, if you were PC Yan and easily impressed, you might have almost thought it was real.

*

He knew what it was. He knew what it was, piece by grisly piece, they were building.

He knew who it was who was doing it.

In his car, driving out of the cross-harbour tunnel that connected the island of Hong Kong to the mainland at Kowloon, Feiffer, his face set, made a left onto Nathan Road and, heading north-west, began travelling finally, at last, unwaveringly, towards China.

12

'Detective Senior Inspector O'Yee?' The voice on the other end of the line was speaking Cantonese. It sounded like the sort of Cantonese you learned in a take-away Chinese food shop in Cambridgeshire. It must have come with the territory. The Fan woman sounded as if her English was out of Charlottesville, NC by Colonel Sanders. The voice said darkly, 'I think you know who this is.' He meant, it was *Us*. 'Harrington gave me your name.'

It was Hal.

O'Yee said pleasantly, also in Cantonese, 'Oh. That's Fred Harrington, is it?'

'No.' There was a pause as Hal thought about it. 'No, *Henry* Harrington.'

O'Yee said, 'Oh.' O'Yee said evenly, 'Never heard of him.'

Hal said, 'Good security, O'Yee.'

There was a long silence.

O'Yee said, 'Thanks, Hal.'

Hal said, 'Ah!' He made a chortling sound. Check in two. Hal said admiringly, 'They said you were good, O'Yee.'

It sure as hell wasn't Len Deighton. Maybe it was. O'Yee said brightly, 'What can I do for you, Hal?'

Hal said, 'Essht!' One name a day was enough. He lowered his voice. 'We believe you've got an op. planned and we'd like to – to –' He thought about it for a moment. 'We'd like to interdict it action-wise.' Hal said quickly, 'You sound American.'

Hal sure as hell didn't sound Cantonese. O'Yee said, 'Strange languages can be deceptive.'

Hal said, not in Cantonese, but in English, 'Yeah.'

O'Yee said quickly, like one of those Russians on television who speak English for no other reason than that the entire viewing audience spoke only English, 'Speak Cantonese, Hal. It is better.' It also meant he was not going to do any voice recognizing. O'Yee said quickly, 'Quick, tell me what it is you want me to do.'

'Call off the op.'

O'Yee said, 'What op?'

'The op you people have got planned for an address which just happens to be the address which we people are interested in which –.' He coughed lightly 'Which just, you know, happens to be the address of the Station headquarters of a certain foreign power who should best remain nameless.' The Russians on television did that too. It wasn't so much security as libel. Hal said, 'OK. If you take my drift . . . ?'

There was a silence.

Hal said, 'Hullo? Are you still there?' Had he said too much? 'O'Yee?'

'Do you mean Room 8, third floor, 78 Peking Road, Hong Bay?'

Hal said, 'Yes!'

'The Ministry Of External Calm, Hong Kong Station, People's Republic Of China Intelligence Service?'

Hal said in English, 'For Christ's sake, O'Yee!'

O'Yee said, 'Because they've gone. We've got an op. planned for where they are now.'

'Where are they now?'

'Don't you know?'

'Of course I know! They're – um –' Hal said, 'They're, um –'

'Yes?' O'Yee said quietly, 'Are you sure you know Harrington? You said Henry Harrington. I always thought it was –'

'I don't know him by his first name! I just know him by his –'

O'Yee said, 'Military rank?'

'Military rank.'

'The Fred Harrington I know never uses his military rank.' If this was what the British Secret Service was like in the Empire no wonder the Empire was crumbling. O'Yee said, to drive the nail to the throat, 'Look, Hal, or whatever your name is, I think if you want some hard information from me about the address of the upcoming op.' – it lost something in Cantonese, but the basic butchery of the expression was still there – 'Then I think you had better give me something to show me you know what you're doing and you are who you say you are.' O'Yee said in a whisper, 'Out here in the cold I can't afford slip-ups.'

'Like what?'

'Like the new address of the Hong Kong Station where, according to you, we've got an op. planned.'

'You've already got it!'

'Have I?' The boy was a babe in the woods. O'Yee said, 'Hal, how long have you been in this business?'

'A couple of years . . .'

'What were you before that? An electrician?' O'Yee said, 'Assume nothing, believe nothing, check everything – get back to me with the address you want me to give you: security. Security. SECURITY!' O'Yee said, 'OK?'

'OK.' Hal said softly, 'Thanks.'

It was nothing. If you couldn't help Us, who could you help?

O'Yee said, 'Right.' O'Yee said, 'This tape will self-destruct in five seconds.'

He hung up.

She was running out of time. On the viewing platform on Hanford Hill overlooking Hong Bay, Miss Fan glanced at her watch and knew she was running out of time. Below her, in the streets, she could see nothing but cars and trucks, trams, buses and wagons, nothing but a million people wedged into a district too small to hold them, part of more people wedged into more districts jam-packed onto an island whose foreign currency and export earnings equalled half the profits for one year of the entire People's Republic. The place hummed with vitality. It was an anachronism, the last gasp of a little nineteenth-century war of colonialization, that, even now, exercised so strong a hold that her government had thought it worth negotiating for as if it was something important like the return of Taiwan or *détente* with Moscow.

Somewhere, down there, part of it all, was her quarry.

She looked again at her watch.

She was running out of time.

She was a slim, athletically-built southern Chinese with good skin and lustrous black hair. She stood very straight by the guard rail on the platform looking down. She was young and pretty, but it was a prettiness with no softness to it. It was simply an arrangement of her features. It mattered to her hardly at all. Here and there around the viewing area there were young men bent on trouble or women, but, even though she was alone and had no one to protect her, they did not approach.

There were three of them: unemployed layabouts. She knew they were there.

It was something about the way she stood, or about her face, or something in her eyes.

They did not approach and, even though she had her back to them, secretly, saying nothing to each other about it, they were each deeply threatened by her presence and, lighting cigarettes and being careful to put the dead matches back in their boxes, they drifted away, out of her orbit.

The mass of men lead lives of quiet desperation.

She did not like the writings of this man Thoreau. She thought him weak and insipid.

She glanced again at her watch.

Touching at the weight the silenced pistol made in her handbag, glancing not at all at the sulking boys in the far corner of the viewing area, she went quickly and resolutely towards the street to make a last, final phone call to O'Yee.

'O'Yee? Herbie Harrington.' Harrington said in what sounded like an accent straight out of Kangaroo Flats, 'How are you, son?'

'I'm well, thanks, Herbie. And you?'

'Just fine.' The accent changed. It became terribly, actually, awfully, doncha-know upper-class English. Harrington said,

'Funny thing –' It came out as 'funn-ee thi-ing . . .' '– but I hear rumours that Ian has been ringing you up and trying to get all sorts of funn-ee information out of you.' The accent went positively P.G. Wodehouse, 'Absolute flannel, of course, but thought I'd run it past you and see –'

'If I saluted?'

'If you saluted.' Harrington said, 'Ha, ha. Well? Did you? Did I see the jolly old hand go to the officer's cap in a snappy one-two-three?' He waited. He said nervously, 'Ha.'

'Ian?'

'Right.'

O'Yee said, 'No.'

'Thought not.' He sounded relieved. The old accent came back. 'Good on ya.' So did the next accent, 'Bit of a bloody relief that.' When one came they all came. Harrington said, 'Eh, what?'

'It was George.'

'*What!*'

'Ha, ha.' He could do them too. O'Yee did a passably good version of a Eurasian cop slowly going out of his mind. O'Yee said, 'Got you there, old son. Actually, it was Hal.'

'That bastard!'

'Right.'

'What did he want?' Harrington said anxiously, 'You didn't tell him anything?'

'What could I tell him? He'd got a rumour the police were mounting a civilian operation against an address he was interested in and he –'

'What address?'

'The new address of the Ministry Of External Calm Station in –'

Harrington said, 'For Christ's sake, not over the phone!' Harrington said, 'You didn't give it to him?'

'I didn't trust him.'

'Quite right.' Harrington's voice dropped to a whisper. Harrington said, 'You've read Le Carré. We all know what a mole is . . .' He said quickly, 'Enough said.' Harrington asked, 'Where is the new Station of the Ministry these days?'

'I don't know.' He was getting Harrington's number fast.

O'Yee said, 'I always thought from what little I've been made privy to in my dealings with you people, that you were the numero uno man who dealt with things like that, Harrington, and certainly not arseholes like Ian or Hal or –'

Harrington said with genuine admiration, 'You're a good man, O'Yee. I've heard that.'

O'Yee said, 'We've got lots of ops. on in the police. I don't know which one happens to be aimed at a building or a place near the new Station if I don't know the address of the new Station.' O'Yee said, 'And, unlike some people who claim to be keeping the world safe for democracy I don't go around spending all my time in inter-office intrigue. I just get on with the real job.' He was getting an awed silence. *Which is keeping the rulers of the slave nations of this Earth from rolling over our wives and children, sisters and mothers in their tanks!*

Too much? There was a silence.

Too much. O'Yee said –

Harrington said with a catch in his voice, 'God bless you, O'Yee.'

'You too, my friend.'

'If only, we had world and time enough –' Harrington said emotionally, 'to meet.'

'Such is life.'

Harrington said, 'I'll get you the address. I'll be back to you within the next few hours.' The Desperate Hours. Harrington, all the accents gone, one soul to another, said, 'Oh, O'Yee, if only people really . . .' He said suddenly, 'I don't even know your first name.' He asked in a whisper, 'What is it?'

O'Yee said, hurt, 'You'll laugh.'

'No, I won't. I promise.' Harrington said sincerely, 'You and me, people like you and me –'

O'Yee said, 'No . . .' He said quickly, 'Just call me "friend".'

'All right, friend.' He didn't laugh. Harrington said, 'Two hours and I'll get back to you.' He said, dripping love, 'Good-bye for now.'

His name?

His *name*?

His name?

Hey presto! Abracadabra!

Hanging up the phone with a bang that almost smashed the instrument to pieces, O'Yee said in triumph, 'My name? My goddamned, bloody name? My name?'

He said softly to the room, '*Houdini*, that's my bloody name!'

He sat back, feeling pleased with himself and awaited patiently the applause.

The mortuary attendant in the hospital had been left-handed: that had been his only mistake – he should have shot him in the other side of the head and left the gun in his left hand. That had been an error. That and the fact that the man Hwa had been driving a car when he had died – he should have realized that it meant that he had money back in Hong Kong, that he had a car of his own and a position – and the NON-VIEWABLE remains would be taken out by an undertaker and the body transferred to a quality casket.

They were the only two mistakes he had made. In his rented station wagon, driving carefully through the traffic towards Burma Road, Colonel Kau, thinking clearly, reviewing it, said softly to himself, 'Yes.'

It had all gone exactly to plan in the hospital with the attendant right up until the very last: the seals, the disposal of the parts, the paperwork, the silence – it had all gone exactly to plan right up to and including the sceptre. Even the killings, the Ping woman, Hwa, all of them, they had all been absurdly easy, and, up to and including the sceptre, it had all gone smoothly and without a hitch.

The only accomplice he had needed during the entire three years of the planning and execution of the operation, had been the mortuary attendant with his saws and knives and sutures and silence, and, right up until the last – literally until the very last coffin – the poor fool had thought it was all legal.

The seals had done that, the seals and the attendant's blind patriotism to China and – he could consider it now that he was on the brink of his new life – the very nature of China itself – the very nature of the secrecy and total government he thought he was serving.

The mortuary attendant had been left-handed. It had been a

mistake to shoot him through the right temple and put the gun in his right hand.

He had been keeping the gun for another death. He had been waiting to find old cartridges for it and reload them with the bullets, caps and powder from the new Winchester rounds; and it had been a mistake to use the gun on him in the railway yards, but he had seen what was in the last coffin and whatever had to be done had had to be done quickly.

He should have remembered the attendant was left-handed. It was the sort of thing he should have made a note of, filed away, had the cool patience to remember before he pulled the trigger.

That and the man Hwa had been his only mistakes.

He thought the chains and weights he had wound around Hwa's coffin before he sank it in the harbour would have been sufficient.

They had come off.

That and the attendant had been his only two mistakes.

Now, at the last, on the last day, there were no more mistakes to be made.

It was not surprising there had been mistakes. *He had planned every bit of it alone.* It was surprising that there had not been more mistakes.

What he had done had been astounding in its planning and execution. What he had done had been –

He stopped thinking about it. There was a red light at the intersection of Great Shanghai Road and Empress Of India Street and, drawing to a halt and applying the handbrake, Colonel Kau lit a cigarette and gazed out of the side window across the harbour.

It had all worked with perfect precision up until the very last coffin, the very last consignment. He glanced up to his rear vision mirror. The last consignment was in the back of the station wagon, with him.

No reviews, no analysis, no self-criticism: all that was in the past.

He had succeeded. Personally, gloriously, self-importantly, he had succeeded. Everything, all the self-effacement, the great common good, the masses – *China* – all that was in the past.

He felt his hands wet on the steering wheel in expectation.

Covered lightly by his summer coat on the passenger seat next to him was a British Special Forces Sterling 9mm sub-machine-gun with a shortened, vented barrel and two clips of ammunition taped together.

He had succeeded. He was in the last hours of the last day.

The light at the intersection changed to green.

Glancing in his rear vision mirror to check the last consignment and moving his coat to conceal one of the curved Sterling magazines that had moved a little when he had stopped, Colonel Kau, about to begin his new life, took off the hand-brake and, putting the station wagon into gear, continued driving carefully and legally towards Burma Road, and, because of the nature of what he carried, avoiding potholes and sudden stops.

It was a little after noon on the last day.

Without taking his eyes off the road, he stubbed the cigarette out carefully in the car's ashtray.

He was in the last hours.

Whatever had gone wrong or been mismanaged or had been cleaned up *ad hoc* was all ancient history.

He smiled to himself.

It was all ancient history.

He was near the end, in the last hours; he was home.

He had done it.

On the phone the Commander said, 'O'Yee, where's Feiffer? What the hell's going on down there?' He didn't wait for the answer. 'I've just come from a meeting with the Security Committee at Government House and been given my orders and my orders include ripping a strip off someone at Yellow-thread Street for putting half the bloody spook services in the Colony into a state of bloody hysteria!' He still didn't wait for a response. The Commander said, 'The bloody Chinese government has made it clear that this business with the coffins is in hand and we're to leave it alone. The bloody British Secret Service, on the other hand, is in a state of total panic that they've got a mole in their ranks and, to top it all, some undercover freak of the first order – someone called Harrington, who evidently spends his time like something out of a Boy's Own Adventure story dressed up as a Chinese beggar, has gone off on his own on some mission laid on by – according to SIS – someone in Yellowthread Street police station!' The Commander said, 'That someone is Feiffer!' He demanded, 'Where is he?' He moderated his tone for an instant. He said in exasperation, 'You haven't got the faintest idea what I'm talking about, have you?'

O'Yee said, 'No, sir.'

'Ever heard of the Ministry Of External Calm? They're the ones who have got the affair in hand!' Someone had said something to him that he had not liked. Someone had told him to back off and mind his own business. The Commander said, 'Not only that, but evidently Feiffer's old friend and confidant John Yin of The Society For Neglected Bones has been ringing up Government House and demanding action and threatening that if he doesn't get it he'll alert the bloody Nationalist Chinese to what the Communist Chinese are doing to the dead and foment the biggest riot this Colony has seen since the war.' The Commander was spluttering. The Commander said as an order, 'When Feiffer – when Detective Chief Inspector Feiffer gets in touch with you, you tell him that according to the Security Committee the bloody Ministry of External Calm has put an *assassin* into Hong Kong to clean up the mess and unless he backs off –' The Commander said, 'God damn it, he even rang the bloody Canton police! The Security Committee have it on tape!' The Commander said, 'Tell him to watch himself!'

'Do you want me to tell him you order him off the case, sir?' In the Detectives' Room, O'Yee, putting on his glasses tried to sound ignorant and dumb. It wasn't difficult. O'Yee said, 'Commander?'

'Tell him to watch himself. Tell him, now, with the future of Hong Kong just about settled, that the last thing anyone wants is –' It rankled him. All his adult life he had been a policeman. The Commander said, 'Tell him –' Someone had pushed. He had not liked it. The Commander said, 'Tell him the Ministry Of External Calm in China – the bloody KGB of the East – has put in a top-flight professional assassin and that he should

143

watch himself.' He said, 'I don't know any more. I don't know who the target is and SIS don't know who the target is and no one – no one – has the faintest idea what's going on except probably Harry Feiffer, and if he knows I don't want him telling people like John Yin and fomenting trouble!' He ordered O'Yee before he could speak, 'You don't have to know what I'm talking about. All you have to do is pass on the message!' He said, 'All right? Have you got that?'

'Yes, sir.'

'Good.' There was a silence. On the line, O'Yee could hear the Commander breathing hard. The Commander said, 'Thanks, O'Yee.' He had been given his orders. The Commander said, 'Tell Harry . . .' There was another pause. He was not a man who liked being shoved. He was not a man who, at the end of a lifetime's work, passed the law of the Colony over to killers. 'Tell him –' He was considering it. He knew what was right. It was ingrained. The Commander said, 'Tell Harry to get on with it and watch his bloody back. Tell him I tried to get what I could from anybody who might know anything and the simple fact of the matter is that nobody does. Tell him –' He sounded upset. 'Tell him all I could find out, all anyone knows – tell him I think the assassin the Ministry Of External Calm has sent in is a *woman*.'

He said with sudden alarm at the silence, 'Hullo? O'Yee? Are you still there?'

'They have sewn dragon's teeth and now they reap the fires of its breath.' On the phone, Miss Fan said in Cantonese to O'Yee, 'No more time now for men to go to the ponds and glades to seek solitude. Now we have reached the last moments and it is time to –'

He heard Auden and Spencer in the charge room coming in with prisoners. O'Yee was silent.

'Find me. Now is the time to –'

O'Yee said softly, 'Miss Fan or whatever your name is –' He had no idea where Feiffer was. O'Yee said in English, 'I have found you. I know who you are.'

'Find me. *Find me! Find me quickly!*'

His hand was trembling on the phone. Outside, in the next

room, he heard Auden and Spencer. He had no idea where Feiffer was. O'Yee said in a whisper, 'I –'

'Find me! *Now!*'

Oh my God. . . At his desk, O'Yee closed his eyes. He listened. He could almost hear her waiting. O'Yee said firmly, 'No. No more.' He said, shaking his head, 'No.'

He said, risking everything, 'You. You come to me.'

He heard Auden say to someone in what he thought was an American accent, 'Yup.'

O'Yee said softly, 'I'm waiting.' He said with his hand wet with perspiration on the receiver, listening hard for the voices of Auden and Spencer, 'Now you: you find me.' He said to her silence, 'I'll be here, waiting.' He had no idea at all where Feiffer was.

He felt his hands tremble.

In the empty room, he hung up and wiped his hand quickly across his mouth.

It was the last day.

At his desk, O'Yee waited.

Deeply, chilled to the bone, he felt afraid.

13

The dead were everywhere. In Customs Warehouse No. 6 at the Lo Wu border a few miles inside Hong Kong, their coffins were stacked in tiers, stowed and arranged, put one on top of the other by a forklift like boats dry berthed in a marina. In the vaulted, silent warehouse, nothing lived. There were rat baits down on the floor and traps for roaches and insects and the air was heavy with the smell of insecticide. There was the smell of camphorwood and varnish, the smell of moisture on the hard stone floors, the smell of death.

In that place, nothing lived.

At the sliding door, turning on the high, overhead neon lights, Preventive Officer Roger K. Morrow (it was on a silver nameplate on his shirt by his shiny Customs Service badge) said with a shrug, 'You want dead Chinese? Take your pick. We've got the full harvest.' The neon lights went on one by one. It was a necropolis. The coffins were arranged like wine bottles in racks, six high, in rows – row after row after row of them. Morrow, his rubber-soled shoes, unlike Feiffer's, not echoing in the awful place as he walked, said, 'In and out. We send them in and out, but mainly in.' The coffin nearest him was an ornate carved affair obviously containing the remains of a man of importance. It was labelled and stickered with coloured Customs tags like a jam jar. Morrow said, 'Every Chinaman who's ever been born wants to go back home to be buried in China.'

He was a young, bearded man with an immaculately pressed uniform. The uniform, by the way he wore it, was obviously important to him. Morrow, flipping over the tags and giving them a quick glance, said casually, 'This one's a character called Lim. He was a millionaire. I know, because he turned up here in the millionaire's hearse and his wife and mistress were both dripping jade and diamonds.' He let the tags fall back into place and gave the coffin lid a rap. 'Anyone home?' He said, smiling, 'You know, the sort of rich, smarmy bastard who wouldn't even nod to you in the street if you worked for him.' He smiled and shrugged again. 'If I liked I could have ordered the coffin opened to check for prohibited substances, but I didn't.' He looked at Feiffer gazing at the rows of caskets. 'Of the percentage of coffins going in and out of China only about point one of one per cent is out. The rest are in.'

'And Owens does those? At the railway station?'

'Owens does his bit for Births, Deaths and Marriages Department. We let him have Customs seals to make things a bit more official for him.' He was a thorough prick. Morrow said, 'It doesn't mean anything. Before his coffins go on to his railway station or wherever it is he works they have to come here and if we feel like it – if I feel like it – his seals don't mean a shit and I can order the coffins to be opened and inspected.' Nothing, to the Customs mind, belonged to anyone but Customs. Everything was at his whim. It was called power. Feiffer wondered for a moment if he struck people the same way. Feiffer, nodding, asked quietly, 'And have you?'

'Have I what?' He was looking at a tag with interest as if, hidden away behind it or between the lines of text, there was something illegal.

'Have you opened any of the coffins that have come in from China in the last three years or so?'

He was about twenty-two years old. Morrow said, 'I haven't been here that long. Before me there was a guy who spent most of his time in the office sleeping. I've only been posted out here for the last six months.' He touched at his beard. It was beautifully, carefully, and recently trimmed. 'I've been trying to catch up on his paperwork.' Talking of it gave him a little more power. He looked impatient. Morrow said, 'I'll have to get on with it, you know.'

'You haven't opened any of the coffins Owens has sent in from Canton?'

'No need.' He shrugged again and laid his hand on the carved dragon of a camphorwood coffin by his side. A thin layer of dust spilled to the floor. He was way behind in his paperwork, or he didn't care. 'We only get about one every two or three weeks in from China. The rest – all these – have to go out from Hong Kong to China and we have enough trouble explaining to the relatives that the regulations have to be met without making more trouble for ourselves by opening coffins coming in.' It didn't quite accord with his image. Morrow said briskly, 'Look, the day Customs stop the Chinese sending their stiffs back home to China to be buried that'll be the day you won't be able to move in Hong Kong for cemeteries.' He didn't like the way the man watched him and listened. He was used to people arguing and protesting with him. Morrow said, 'What sort of coffin are you looking for anyway?' He said, taking his hand off the casket and glancing back to the door to signal that he had work waiting, 'Even if we're holding a coffin in from China you think you may want I don't know if I've got the authority to have it opened just on suspicion.'

'I have.'

Morrow said, 'Have you?' He looked dubious.

'I'm looking for a small coffin, the coffin maybe of a child – someone who died in China – a Hong Kong national – with no relatives.'

'Children always have relatives.' It irritated him. Morrow said, 'We haven't got anything like that.'

'Sent in in the last week.'

'No.'

'Sealed by Owens at the Canton Military Hospital for interment in Hong Kong, complete with all the necessary papers.'

Morrow said, 'No.'

'Or a huge casket, something very big.' It had to be either very big or very small. The thing it contained, the thing that the murdered mortuary attendant had seen that had set the whole chaos going, had to have been put in a coffin that was either under-sized or over-sized. It was something that could not have been disguised as part of a body, not by weight or shape or configuration. It was the last thing, the thing that made the assemblage of human parts what they were. It had to have come in in something special. Feiffer said anxiously, 'Anything at all.'

'No.'

'What about something you've already sent on to Owens, something that's already at the railway station in Kowloon for collection?'

'Ask Owens.'

'I'm asking you!' Feiffer, tightening his hands into fists to control himself, said tensely, 'Owens is in Canton at the moment. I can't ask him until he comes back late tonight.'

He spent his life going through other people's property. The sensation of power as he examined their baggage and personal possessions as they stood there looking at him at an airport or a dock had never waned. Morrow said, 'The job of Customs is to expedite the entry and export of goods of a non-prohibited nature and to –' He saw Feiffer advance on him. Morrow said, stepping back, 'We don't even look at bloody Owens' stuff. We're not allowed to – all right? There's an arrangement with the Chinese Customs people that anything he seals is OK and if we started tampering with them they'd start tampering with us and no one would ever get any work done.' He was losing his power by the moment. In his own world he was a cog. 'Christ Almighty, just the bloody paperwork on these things means it takes weeks to get one across the border into China. At least with Owens going into Canton it means we can get the China to Hong Kong coffins out of our way quickly.'

'*Have you sent anything to Owens in the last week?*'

'No. Owens only hands out the Chinese dead from his bloody railway station. We haven't sent him any Chinese dead!'

'What about other nationalities?' He was asking, 'Have you got anything to declare?' Morrow, the innocent passenger, was saying no.

Morrow said, 'Like who?'

It clicked. He knew how it worked. Feiffer, coming close to the man and then stepping back a pace to set a distance between them, said suddenly, 'I have to warn you that if you have or are about to make a false declaration I have the power to arrest you and have you charged with –'

'I sent out a box containing the remains of two dead Swedish sailors!' Morrow, wetting his lips, stepping back a pace, said, shrugging, changing his tone, 'I – there was a wooden packing-case sort of thing came in from China with the remains of two Swedish sailors in it for cremation. Owens does the Chinks – that's his brief. It didn't concern Owens.' He said suddenly, 'Owens has got too much bloody power already for someone who just works for Births, Deaths and Marriages – and I just – I exercised my power and signed the remains out here.'

He was a thorough prick. Feiffer, his mouth hard, said in a whisper, 'Were they remains that Owens had certified?'

'In theory, yes.'

'What do you mean "in theory"? *Yes or bloody no?*'

'Yes!'

'Then what the hell do you mean by signing them out here and not sending them on to the railway station?'

'I told you! They weren't Chinese! They were the remains of two Swedish seamen who'd gone overboard in the Pearl River and got cut to pieces by propellers! They'd been in the water for a week –'

Feiffer said, 'And the remains were marked Non Viewable, am I right?'

'Yes.' Morrow, running his tongue across his lips, said in protest, 'It's all right. They weren't Chinese, they were Europeans. They were –' He said desperately, 'They weren't going to be buried anyway. That's the sort of thing Owens does: all this Chinese shit about proper burial and lying with your ancestors and all that stuff!' Like all men who spent their days at borders gazing at the people who crossed those borders he had conceived a terrible hatred for anything strange or foreign or alien. Morrow said, 'These were people who were going to be cremated and their ashes sent home to Sweden!' He said, 'Christ, they were both in the same box. That was how little ordinary people – normal people – care about all this

Chink death stuff – all I did was sign the box out to an undertaker who turned up here to collect it!' Morrow said with sudden vehemence, 'I hate that bastard Owens. You've met him. Puffed-up little Taffy bastard! He spends all his bloody time all over the world riding around on bloody trains!'

He had not even been bribed. All the man who picked up the case containing the mincemeat of the two dead Swedes would have had to have done to get what he wanted was grovel. For what was in the case along with the ruined flesh, it was little enough to pay. Feiffer said, 'Which crematorium did he claim to represent?'

'He had all the papers all made out properly!'

'Which bloody crematorium?' It was all too late.

'The Hong Bay crematorium on Burma Road!' Morrow said, 'I checked! I do my job properly! I checked all his papers! According to the regulations I have full discretion to act on my own –'

'The bloody Burma Road Crematorium has been closed for six months! The entire area around it is listed for redevelopment!' Was it possible? Was it possible that, right at the end, they had had to – finally, at last – do something obvious? Feiffer said urgently, 'When? When did you let this case out? Yesterday? The day before? *When?*'

'An hour and a half ago –' He saw Feiffer's face. It was not a face he recognized. It was the face he himself had always dreamed of being able to put on when, going through a sweating, nervous passenger's baggage, he had, at last, found something desperately illegal.

Morrow was afraid, 'What is it? Have I –' He called after the running man, 'I didn't know I wasn't allowed to do –' He began to chase after him.

In the dead, echoing, chill room, his uniform getting filthy as he banged into first one casket in its rack and then another in his haste to catch up, Morrow shouted in sudden alarm and entreaty, 'Please! Please! *I didn't know I was doing anything wrong!*'

At the address in his sealed orders there was a truck waiting for the final delivery. It was in an alley off General Gordon Street on the eastern side of the district, near the intersection of Soochow Road and Khartoum Street. The keys were under the fender of the truck, held in place by a strip of tape.

It was for the final delivery of the completed, assembled goods to the docks. In the glovebox there were all the necessary papers correctly made out and stamped with what looked like a perfect copy of the rubber stamp of the Hong Bay Docks Customs Section. In the passenger's seat, the Captain folded them carefully and put them in his pocket.

It was a one-ton truck, large enough for his squad to make the short trip he planned in the back without discomfort.

One last trip. As the driver got in beside him and put the keys in the ignition, the Captain, to encourage him, smiling, patted him gently on the arm.

They were all thinking of getting on the plane for home.

There was no need this time for the Captain to consult his map or give directions: they had been making deliveries to the address they were going to, non-stop for the last two days.

The Captain, touching at his pistol in its holster and still smiling, said softly in Mandarin, ' "*Pu ju 'hu hsüeh, pu tê 'hu tzu*": If you do not enter a tiger's den, you cannot get his cubs.'

The legend on the side of the truck read in large Chinese characters CELESTIAL LUCK MOVING COMPANY. The irony was not lost on him.

The Captain, nodding to the driver to start the engine, said softly, to no one in particular, 'Nothing that matters has gone wrong.'

He looked at his watch.

The Captain, banging on the back wall of the driver's compartment to signal his squad that they were about to move off, yelled loudly above the sound of the engine turning over, 'Stay alert! Now particularly! *Stay alert!*'

He touched at his pistol in his belt and checked that it was still there.

In the Detectives' Room, Auden, glancing around, said, 'Where's Harry?'

In the corner of the room O'Yee said tightly, 'Shut up, Phil.'

Both Auden and Spencer were back in their street clothes. Spencer had a faint glassy look to his eyes. Around Auden's eyes there were still traces of make-up. There was a spot of beard glue below his ear. O'Yee, watching the open door, said without looking at them, 'Don't sit down.' There was nothing on any of the desks in the room – no papers – everything had been cleared. O'Yee said, 'In the top drawer of your desk.' He watched as Auden went to the desk and pulled open the drawer and saw his magnum. It had been recently cleaned and oiled. By it was a box of fifty rounds of ammunition.

O'Yee said as an order to Auden's puzzled face, 'Load it!'

He wore his own Detective Special in its upside-down Berns-Martin shoulder holster. He glanced towards the open door.

O'Yee said with no room for argument or protest, 'Now! Do it now!'

Twenty-one, twenty-two, twenty-three... The shortened Sterling held thirty-two rounds in its curved magazine, loaded by a special charger. Alone, in the empty room, Colonel Kau, loading the weapon not with the charger but carefully, by hand, one round at a time, stopped at thirty to keep the magazine under an even tension that would not jam the action. The other two taped-together magazines he had also loaded by hand one round at a time, he put carefully into the hip pocket of his trousers, making sure that the lips were up and un-snagged.

He had done it. It was almost over. The thing – the creature he had put together piece by piece was in the next room, waiting. It had waited a very long time. It had been made from pieces of the dead. It lived. It had lived a very long time and now, in there, in the semi-darkness of a windowless room, it still lived.

He checked the position of the top nine-millimetre jacketed cartridge in the lips of the gun's magazine, turning it in the faint light so that the brass case glittered.

For eight hundred million people – for every soul in the entire People's Republic Of China – the creature lived.

Satisfied, he pushed the magazine into the housing at the side of the gun until he heard the magazine retaining catch snap shut. He did not slap the magazine in hard: they only did that in sensational American movies for the effect. In reality, all it did was distort the magazine and make the weapon unreliable.

He listened. He heard no sound at all.

In the next room, the creature he had constructed lived.

He had done it.

It had taken a lot of time and effort and he had killed a great number of people one way or the other, but now, finally, at last, it was almost over.

In the dark, silent stone room in which he waited, there was almost no air. He felt a drop of sweat run down the side of his face.

He listened.

He waited.

He drew back the cocking handle on the side of the shortened sub-machine-gun and, his hand shaking a little in expectation, let it go.

The bolt flew forward and chambered a round.

In the silent room, echoing, it came as a sudden, jarring *Snap!*

In the pathology laboratory in the mortuary, Doctor Macarthur, peering hard at the display screen of his electron microscope, said in a whisper, 'God . . . !' He had one of his inevitable Gauloise Disque Bleu cigarettes burning away on the corner of the microscope screen bench and he picked it up and blew a haze of smoke from it onto the information up on the display window and watched it billow.

He had samples of the earths from Soong's private cemetery in the machine. He looked at the breakdown of what those earths contained and said softly, 'God damn . . .'

A sceptre. Harry Feiffer, at the graveside, had said that the shadow on the linen shroud had been a sceptre. At the time Macarthur had had no idea what he meant.

It was not all earth. In the specimen there were traces of other things, other elements, other natural products.

There were ochres and cobalts, pumices, vegetable matter, colours.

He punched up a higher magnification and, tapping the keys on his console with the cigarette still in his mouth, isolated just one of the trace elements on the display.

He turned it from a linear display to a visual one and saw in detail, throughout the earth, permeating it, part of it, in it pore by pore from the two burials, traces of a heavy brown matter.

The shadow on the shroud had not been a sword at all. It had been a sceptre.

Brown earth. That was what the major trace through the specimen was: brown . . . earth.

Terra . . . cotta.

He saw another speck. He knew without checking the spectrometer tied in to the microscope what it was.

Gold. It was a single fleck of gold.

Macarthur said softly in the haze of blue smoke and the humming of the machine, 'Christ Almighty . . .'

He sat staring at the screen in silence, smoking, trying to think.

He began tapping out instructions to the machine carefully, symbol by symbol, so there would be no possibility of a mistake.

Feiffer already knew what it was. It was coming to Macarthur a little at a time, according to scientific method, but the results would be the same.

He could hardly believe it.

Tapping out instructions, lighting another cigarette from the burning tip of the first, Macarthur, his eyes glued to the display screen, said softly, incredulously, 'Christ Almighty, I don't believe it – it couldn't be *that* . . . !'

He had seen all the seals on all the coffins when they had broken them open.

They were perfect, real. They were seals put on the coffins by a representative of the Hong Kong government with the approval and supervision of the government of the People's Republic Of China and they were, without doubt, on cursory, on general, or even on close, minute examination, one hundred per cent genuine, and he did not understand how Kau or the Colonel or whatever he called himself had done it.

By the door of the truck, the Captain, banging on the side to alert his squad, called out in Mandarin, 'Out! Out! Bring your weapons!'

There was no one around. The truck stood out in the open, outside a wire mesh fence, and all he could see around him were deserted, abandoned, shell-like buildings. He saw the driver climb out of his cab and come around with his Ingram in his hand, drawing back the cocking handle as he went.

The rear door of the truck slid open and, without pausing, his squad was jumping down to the ground with their guns held at port.

'Secure the area!' He saw them fan out around the truck, keeping apart, crouching down, their gun barrels pointing ahead.

There was no danger. The area was empty and deserted. There was no wind and the Captain, listening hard, heard no sound at all.

'Bolt cutters!' He had a key for the padlock on the gate of the wire fence, but he had no intention of taking the truck in for the last time and being caught inside the compound with the gate padlocked against him.

He heard a snap as one of the squad brought up the cutters and cut through the bolt.

'Leave the truck here.' He looked ahead to the deserted buildings. He thought for a moment to leave the driver there as a rearguard and then changed his mind.

It was the last time. He was going to risk no one. Tonight, after this was over, everyone was going home and he wanted no widows awaiting him.

The Captain said, 'Everyone, everyone goes with me.' He saw the driver look dubious. 'If it's all right we can bring the truck up later.' He had the papers for the ship in his pocket. The Captain said, 'I've got the papers.'

He drew a breath. For the last two days he had been taking orders from a man he had never met, a man who had the power to seal coffins in China with the seals of an unfriendly government.

The Captain said quickly, 'Right, straight in!'

Inside the building directly in front of them he was waiting:

the man with all the orders – Kau, the Colonel: the man with the power.

Moving forward, his eyes darting quickly from one member of his squad to another as he went, he wondered how the man had done it.

He wondered how, over a period of at least three years, day by day, action by action, undetectably, he had succeeded in deceiving and using for his own personal ends the governments and bureaucratic machines of at least two of the most powerful and well-organized nations in the world.

Colonel Kau –

He wondered who he was.

14

'His name is Colonel Kau Kam Sung and up until a week ago he was the Hong Kong and Canton Station head of the Ministry Of External Calm covert section – the Chinese Secret Service.' In the Detectives' Room, standing facing them, Miss Fan said in a neutral English that to O'Yee seemed to have lost even the faintest trace of the Southern accent, 'During the last three years, illegally, he has been using the full facilities of the Ministry's document and seals forgery section for his plan and now he is running and he cannot be located.' She was only a small girl in her mid- to late twenties. Her presence in the room was everywhere. She carried in her hand a large leather handbag. It looked heavy. She carried it with no effort. She wore no jewellery nor rings. In black slacks and a light long-sleeved black blouse, she was like a cat. Her eyes stayed fixed on O'Yee's face.

Auden said, 'What plan?' He looked at Spencer watching her. 'Harry's bodies?' He saw O'Yee glance at the heavy handbag. Auden said, 'Who the hell are you?' He got no reply. He knew who she was. Auden said in a whisper, 'God Almighty . . .'

O'Yee said evenly, 'I don't know where he is.'

'The Station has gone.' Miss Fan looked hard at O'Yee, reading his face. She was not so much standing as balancing on the balls of her feet. Auden's hand touched at the butt of his gun. He knew she saw the movement. Miss Fan said, 'Christopher, you are my only hope to find him.'

O'Yee said, 'No.'

Spencer said quietly, 'What about your own people?'

'Colonel Kau was our own people. He recruited personnel in Hong Kong as he needed them.' Miss Fan's eyes were boring into O'Yee's. Miss Fan said without emotion, 'The people who may have been close to him here in Hong Kong – the people he recruited for tasks, his regulars – are all missing. He probably killed them.' She saw Spencer's hand touch at his belt where his gun was. She turned her head slightly towards him and the movement stopped. Miss Fan said, 'The Chinese People's Republic has negotiated peacefully for the return of Hong Kong at the appropriate time. It has all been settled.' She looked at Auden. 'You have no need to be afraid of me.'

O'Yee said firmly, 'I don't know where he is.'

'You have been trying to find out.' Miss Fan said tightly, 'You know who I am.'

O'Yee shook his head. O'Yee said definitely, 'I haven't been able to find out anything. I couldn't find you. I couldn't find him. I don't know the new address of the goddamned Ministry in Hong Kong and even if I did –'

Miss Fan said abruptly, 'If you did it would be your duty to tell me!'

'Are you armed?'

Miss Fan said, 'That is none of your affair.'

'If you are armed with a concealable weapon in this Colony without a permit –'

'This Colony is in its last breaths!' Whatever she was, she was a professional. Anyone else would have gripped the bag a little tighter or glanced down to it. She did neither. Miss Fan, seeing Auden take a step forward, said without force, 'Stand still.' There was the faintest tic at the side of her eyes. It was not fear. It was a terrible tightness held hard in check. Miss Fan said urgently, 'Tell me what you know!'

'I don't know anything!' O'Yee, shaking his head, said, 'I don't know where Kau is and I didn't know where you were and I don't know where –' O'Yee said, 'All we've got is your word for what you're saying!' O'Yee said suddenly, angrily,

'Why me? Why the hell did you pick on me to find your goddamned traitor? Why me?'

'Because you would.'

'Well, I couldn't!' O'Yee, still shaking his head, trying to decide what to do, said, 'No. No, this isn't right. This isn't the way this sort of thing should happen. The people you should be dealing with are –' The people she should have been dealing with were George and Ian and Hal and goddamned Abbott and Costello. O'Yee, desperate, said, 'I can't do things like this! I haven't got the power or the right!' All he had was the gun in her bag. All he had was a minor weapons arrest. All he had – O'Yee said, 'What the hell did you mean when you said the fate of the bloody world rested on it?'

'Your world. This world.'

'This world is finished and settled. The Chinese government and the British government have –'

Miss Fan said, 'If you do not tell me where Kau is I can guarantee you that within a week there will be riots and armed conflicts on the streets of Hong Kong and at the border.'

'How? *Why?* How do you know that?' O'Yee said, 'What the hell is Kau doing? You're here to kill him, aren't you?'

Miss Fan said, 'Yes.'

'What the hell has he done?'

'By now I believe your man Detective Chief Inspector Feiffer knows.'

'I can't get in touch with Detective Chief Inspector Feiffer! I don't know where he is!' O'Yee said, 'Tell me what he knows!'

'I cannot.' Miss Fan said, 'In case he does not know.'

'In case he does not know *what?*' O'Yee, looking to Auden, said as an order, 'Phil –'

Spencer said, 'What did he do? Kau? What is he sending in the coffins apart from parts of bodies?'

'Apart from parts of bodies, nothing.' Miss Fan, drawing a breath, said, 'He had a brief to travel all over China and into Hong Kong and the special administrative areas around Canton – into military bases, military hospitals, anywhere. He had the right to use the full facilities of any government department and to institute and execute any operation he might have thought appropriate without reference to a higher power. In Honan province he murdered a Hong Kong woman named Ping Kit-Ling and arranged to have her body shipped back to Hong Kong via the Canton Military Hospital. We believe that he was also responsible for the deaths of other Hong Kong citizens for the same purpose – these people he chose, not at random, but with particular reference to the fact that they had no living relatives and would be buried with their caskets unopened.'

She was saying too much. She paused.

'We believe he arranged the deaths in such a way that the remains would be unviewable because of the nature of their injuries.' Miss Fan said, 'He was able to do this because his position automatically meant that he would receive full details of any Hong Kong citizens travelling in China together with copies of their passports or travelling papers and their vetting information.' She was giving it away a little at a time, reading O'Yee's face. The moment she saw confusion there – alarm – she would have to stop. Miss Fan said, 'He, in concert with an employee in the Canton Military Hospital, then dismembered these bodies and –' She saw the look. '– the employee believed he was working legally. Kau showed him his authorization from the Ministry and the employee thought he was aiding the designs of the State.' They knew about the dead morgue attendant. By now, they must have known. Miss Fan said, 'When the employee realized that this was not the case – because of something he saw – the Colonel faked his suicide and murdered him.' She glanced at Auden. Under his coat he carried a Colt Python .357 magnum with a six-inch barrel. Miss Fan said to him, 'You know guns. He made the mistake of using modern ammunition with a very old pistol.' Her eyes flicked to O'Yee. 'The Canton police had no trouble in discovering that the employee's suicide was a badly botched, hastily executed murder.'

O'Yee said, shaking his head, 'I don't understand any of it.'

'His brief was wide ranging. He was able to travel anywhere in China. Anywhere! Any province. He was able with his credentials to do anything! These coffins – these dead people – these people – ordinary, poor people – these are people he *killed!*'

'*Why?*'
'For his plan.'
O'Yee said, '*What plan?*'
'*Do you know where he is?*'
'Maybe!'
'If you know you must say!'

'Why? Why must I say?' O'Yee, deciding, said suddenly, 'No.' O'Yee said, 'Miss Fan, I have reason to believe that you are in possession of a firearm with intent to endanger life contrary to the Firearms Act and it is my duty to ask you to –'

Miss Fan said, 'In the coffins, over the last three years, he has been smuggling sections of an object out of China into Hong Kong! By now, if my information is correct, if our estimate of him is correct, your commanding officer, Mr Feiffer, will know what it is!'

O'Yee said, 'What is it!?'

'It is –' Miss Fan asked, 'Christopher, please, do you know where Kau can be found?' The tic around her eye was going. They saw her hand tighten on the leather strap of her handbag. Miss Fan said with difficulty, 'It is – if the – if it is not –' Miss Fan said with an attempt at a smile, 'All men are not equally fit subjects for civilization.' Miss Fan said, 'Thoreau!' She looked at O'Yee. Miss Fan said precisely, 'Over the last three years, he has taken, piece by piece from its rightful owners, hidden in coffins containing the dismembered and desecrated bodies of the poor and the lonely and the unwanted – he has taken China's heart!' She said desperately, so softly that they had to strain to hear her, 'Please, please – *tell me where he is!*'

'Hotel Baker Three –'

. . . . .

'Hotel Baker Three –'

It was a dead spot. From the speaker on his car radio there was only static.

'*Hotel Baker Three to Base –*'

There was nothing. In his parked car, Feiffer, gazing across at the truck a little outside the wired-off compound of the redevelopment area, put the microphone back into its cradle and kneaded at his hands. There was nothing moving in the area, in the absence of wind, no sound or motion at all.

'*Hotel Baker Three* —'

There was nothing. His forehead was dripping sweat. He hung the microphone up again and ran his hand across the car seat beside him.

'*Hotel Baker Three to Base!*'

He was wasting his time.

Hotel Baker Three was the Station workhorse car. It was the only one that carried no heavy weapons in its trunk as standard equipment.

He was afraid. He felt his heart pounding in his chest. It was as if, somehow, he had come to be the last of a dying breed in a dying place surrounded by the dead.

'*Hotel Baker Three to Base* —'

He knew what they had in their coffins. He knew what it was, piece by piece, they had put together. For a moment, Feiffer thought of his wife and son.

There were no heavy weapons in the car at all.

Wiping his forehead with his hand and then the hand itself on the leatherette seat beside him, he got out of the car drawing his revolver and began walking slowly towards the truck.

He saw the driver, taking the point, jump back and bring up his Ingram. The Captain said as an order, 'Easy!'

It was only a rat or an insect. The derelict stone building was full of them. He looked up and saw the laths in the ceiling hanging down. The building was falling apart.

The Captain said again, gently, 'Easy . . . easy . . .' He motioned for the squad behind and around him to slow down and draw a breath. They were in a long dank-smelling corridor: he did not want to wait there too long. The Captain, nodding to the driver to continue, said in Mandarin, 'All right. Straight ahead.'

He knew where they were going.

He listened. He heard no sound ahead of him.

He knew the Colonel was there.

The Captain, glancing behind him to make sure their backs were safe, said encouragingly, 'Go, go.' He touched at the safety catch of his Browning and slipped it forward with no sound at all.

The Captain, moving through the corridor of the empty building with his squad, said softly in Mandarin, 'It's only another few feet.'

On the phone, the Commander said in a whisper, 'My God, are you sure?'

He had not known who else to ring. Standing over the electron microscope in the pathology lab with the phone gripped hard in his hand, Macarthur said definitely, 'Yes, I'm sure.'

'You're certain it's that? There couldn't be any mistake?' He sounded desperate. The Commander, drawing a breath, trying to think, said, 'You haven't told anyone else?'

'I didn't know who else to ring. I think Harry Feiffer knows, but I —' Macarthur said, 'I didn't know who else to ring.' Macarthur said, 'It was the colour of the paint flecks — the pigment — yellow.' He asked, 'Will you contact Peking or —'

'You're sure it couldn't be anything else?' The Commander said without waiting for an answer, 'Oh my God . . . !' He was trying hard to think what to do. Nothing came.

The Commander said quietly, thinking aloud, incapable of any thought at all, aghast, 'Oh my God . . . what the hell am I going to do?'

The padlock on the gate of the wire fence had been broken with bolt cutters. They were in there. In the deserted and derelict area there was no sound or movement at all. It was a place for the dead.

Alone, with no one in the world knowing where he was, Feiffer began walking towards the stone building directly ahead of him with his gun held loosely at his side.

His heart had stopped pounding. He was moving in slow motion.

He thought, sometimes, at night when he was alone, of how Shanghai had ended and what it had done to his father who had spent his life there. Like the dodo or the carrier-pigeon, he had become extinct.

He thought for a moment of his wife's face and his son.

Closing the wire gate behind him, he began walking towards the steps at the entrance to the grey, stone, blank, windowless building and, glancing for a moment to the high, rusted black chimney that protruded from its centre, reaching the steps, mounted them and went inside.

'In Shensi province —!' Miss Fan shouted, 'In Shensi province, they unearthed the burial mounds of the Emperor Ch'in Shih-huang-ti: the first Emperor of China! There, in pits, in lines, ranks, columns, tiers, they found an entire buried army of effigies — of terra cotta figures! They found archers, soldiers, cavalry, row after row of figures done in clay each modelled on a living soldier of the third-century emperor, each — all of them — with perfect, exact detail — all —'

Spencer said, 'I read about it. It was the greatest archaeological find of —'

'— each man, each soldier, each officer arranged as he would have been in life protecting the great burial mound of the Emperor, each standing like the dead slaves of the Egyptian pharaohs according to his rank and his position and his order in life and society and —' Miss Fan said, 'It is said that they were created over twenty years at the command of the Imperial palace and that —' She was on the edge of losing control, saying too much, giving too much away for nothing in return. 'Seven thousand of them! Seven thousand perfect, irreplaceable figures in a complete time capsule, disturbed only here and there by grave robbers, all armed, some of them set like machines with booby-trapped crossbows to protect the dead Emperor's spirit from marauders and despoilers, all —' Miss Fan said, 'He was there when it was found — Colonel Kau — he was there when they opened up the first pits and saw the soldiers set up in rows! He was there when —'

Spencer said, 'My God, it's one of the statues!'

Miss Fan said, 'No.' She looked at O'Yee. Miss Fan said, 'Christopher, *please*! If you know where he is —'

'I don't!'

Spencer said, 'Then what? If it isn't one of the statues — if he hasn't been sending in parts of one of the statues as parts of the bodies in the coffins then what has he been –'

Auden said, 'Treasure.'

Miss Fan said, 'Christoper, we studied you and read your file and learned everything there is to learn about you.' She had the bag gripped tight in her hands. Her hands were shaking. For a moment O'Yee thought she was going to reach forward and grasp him by the shoulders. 'You're part Chinese! You're one half Chinese! You're a man who straddles two worlds! You, with your Thoreau and your –' Miss Fan, dismissing Auden with contempt, said, 'Yes, it's treasure, but nothing you or anyone like you would ever think was treasure! It is a treasure that only a Chinese would think was treasure! It *is* China! It is –' She said, trembling, '*Tell me where Colonel Kau is now!*'

'*I don't know!*'

Auden said, 'If it isn't treasure then who the hell is he going to sell it to? Who the hell are the bloody people digging it up? If only a Chinese would understand it who the hell are –'

O'Yee said suddenly, 'The Nationalists. The Nationalists on Taiwan, the anti-Communist Chinese: it's them, isn't it? That's who the people digging up the coffins are. *Isn't it?*'

Miss Fan said, 'Yes!' Miss Fan said, 'Yes! Yes! Yes!' She had her hands out in front of her appealing to him. Miss Fan said, 'Hong Kong is going. There will be no place left for them on the mainland of China. Piece by piece, they will dissolve, become nothing, become less than Chinese. With Hong Kong gone, the Americans and the British and the Chinese will form a unity, a triad in Asia based not on colonialism and exploitation, but on mutual commerce and trust, and the Nationalists, the fossils from the days of Chiang Kai Shek and Mao, will dissolve away to nothing!' Miss Fan said with her fists clenched, 'If Kau is not stopped – if this plan is not stopped –'

O'Yee said as an order to respond, 'What is it he's got from the excavations?'

Miss Fan said, 'I cannot say.' She entreated him, 'Tell me where he is.'

'*What is it he's got?*'

'I cannot tell you!' The phone on O'Yee's desk rang, and, a moment before O'Yee snatched it up and said urgently,

'Harry?', Miss Fan begged him, 'Tell me where he is so I can kill him quickly!'

It was Harrington. Harrington, without pausing for O'Yee to identify himself, shouted, 'O'Yee, you dirty bastard! You dirty little half-caste bastard, you've lied to me!'

O'Yee shouted back down the line, 'Harrington?'

'You dirty, lying, cheating bastard, you're working for bloody Ian or Hal or George and I bloody well, fucking fell for it like a ton of bricks, didn't I?' Harrington said with pure undiluted hatred, 'I believed you. I believed that you were on my side and that you had the best interests of our bloody side at heart, but, just like all the rest of them, you lied and lied and bloody lied!' Harrington shrieked, 'You lying bastard, you knew all the time where the new Station for the fucking Chinese Secret Service was being set up – you half-Chinese goddamned traitor, you're probably one of them yourself! You knew it was the bloody Hong Bay Crematorium on Burma Road – you bloody knew and all this was some sort of plan you hatched with George and Ian and Hal and all the gentlemen traitors and fucking poofs in SIS to discredit me because –'

O'Yee said tightly, 'I didn't know.'

'No? Didn't you?' Harrington said, 'No? Didn't you? Well I'm not fucking hanging around when the shooting starts. I'm not hanging around when Colonel Kau and his squad of killers or whoever they are, meet up with your little man and I'm not –'

'What the hell are you talking about?'

'I'm talking about –' Harrington said on the edge of hysteria, 'Let him die! I don't care! I'm saving my own skin! Let him fucking die!'

O'Yee said, 'Who? Let who die?' O'Yee said, 'What my "little man"? What –' O'Yee said, 'Oh my God!' O'Yee said in horror, 'Oh my God – *Feiffer!*'

The phone rang. It was the Commander. He had decided. He had been a policeman in Hong Kong too long to give it all up at the end. The Commander, two years off retirement, said quickly, 'One question. Have you or have you not any idea where these people are who have been going around digging up goddamned coffins and killing people?' He said tightly, 'Yes or no?'

O'Yee said, 'Yes.'

'All right.' He sounded hard, tensed, like stone. The Commander said, 'Then listen, understand. I can't help you. I can't officially call anyone else in to help. I can't do anything that might involve the Hong Kong government or the Chinese government or any organ of either of those governments – do you understand that?'

O'Yee said, 'Yes.'

'It's you. It's just you and whoever you've got to help you: that's all.' The Commander said, 'OK? Understood?' The Commander said, 'I am now giving you and the people at your command – and only them – a direct order – *do you understand what I'm saying?*'

'Yes.'

'Good.' The Commander said, 'Detective Senior Inspector O'Yee – Christopher – if you know where those people are, take them out. Take them out for the murder of the coffin repository owner Kan or take them out for disturbing sacred ground, or take them for any crime they've committed in Hong Kong, but take them out!' The Commander, on familiar ground, feeling his strength returning, flowing back, said as a direct, unarguable command, 'Now! *Take them out now!*'

15

In the car Auden said for the last time, 'What is it? If it isn't one of the statues then what is it?'

It was the heart of China. It was the six and a half foot tall, yellow-sceptred and armoured effigy of the first Emperor of China, Ch'in Shih-huang-ti. It was *the* statue. It was the symbol of the moment in China when the Chinese had turned from barbarity to civilization. One single glittering climax seventeen centuries ago – the moment when a king had merged a nation into one people and became an Emperor. It was the greatest of the tomb figures from Mount Li in Shensi province – the one the archaeologists still dug for – it was Ch'in Shih-huang-ti: The Blessed First Sovereign Of China.

In the chapel of the crematorium the figure stood before the deconsecrated, ruined altar, bathing in the light from cracked and broken, stained and coloured glass windows all around it. It was perfect: even from the organ loft high above the body of the chapel Feiffer, crouched down, could see the features of the face and each of the links and plates of the armour, the outline of the dragon sceptre, the hands, even the fingernails. It was the greatest masterpiece of the sculptors who had constructed each of the funeral figures that protected the dead Emperor: it was the final great effigy of the Emperor himself at the head of his troops. Piece by piece, over three years, it had come into the Colony to be re-assembled. He had seen photos of the ranks and tiers and columns of armed terracotta men the archaeologists and sinologists had excavated from the site – they were nothing. They were mere pawns to the Emperor's king. It took his breath away. At the ruined altar as the squad of armed men watched, he saw an older man stand on a chair and, raising it above the wonderfully coiffured head of the creature, place the great crown upon the head.

It was not terracotta like the rest of the figure, not painted and picked out in the colours of the Empire and the colour of the Emperor: the Imperial yellow – it was of the finest glazed porcelain. In the light it glittered and flashed. It was a bicorn hat, a sort of mortar board, hanging down from it strands of the finest silk that was not silk at all, but glass. In the light, as the older man moved it, it exploded into a brilliance of power and command.

So far, at the excavations the archaeologists had found seven thousand figures. They were nothing. Even the greatest of them: terracotta generals with real swords and crossbows and batons, were nothing.

Feiffer said in a whisper, 'My God, it's real.' The generals and the soldiers had all been armed with real weapons. The figure of the Emperor held his sceptre in his left hand. Feiffer said in a whisper, 'My God, it's real!' It was the sceptre of China. It was real. The crown had come in in the last casket, in the box containing the remains of the dead Swedes. It was that that the morgue attendant had seen. It was that that had made him realize what it was he had been helping with. It was that that had made him realize what was being taken. It was that that had gotten him killed. It caught the light. In the older man's hands it shimmered with life. Feiffer, trying to see more, saw the squad of soldiers, their eyes devouring the sight, step back. They were all armed with automatic weapons. The muzzles of the weapons were down. They stared at the creature on the altar shaking their heads. They were the Nationalists. They were a Special Forces Squad from Taiwan. Hong Kong was going and, with it, their only toe-hold on mainland China. They were becoming a back number – their island of Taiwan a footnote to history, a backwater – all their Chineseness being dissipated and taken from them in strokes of pens. They had the symbol of their race. They had the funeral effigy of the first Emperor of China – their Emperor – and they were taking it with them when they went. They seemed wary of the man at the altar: he was the one who had got it for them – God only knew who he was. God only knew what power he had or once had. On the floor Feiffer saw a long wooden crate laid out ready for loading with open Hong Kong government Customs seals ready to be closed and impressed. They were too far away to make out, but he knew, just like the ones on the coffins, they were real.

They were not real. They had been done, not by the Royal Mint, but by the Chinese Mint. The man stood down from his chair. Feiffer saw the soldiers' attention still on the great effigy. He saw the older man reach down into the crate and take something from the packing there. It was a shortened Sterling sub-machine-gun. The effigy, for almost two thousand years, had stood, so the story went, in the actual funeral chamber of the dead Emperor surrounded by a miniature of that Empire: the mountains and plains all jade and hardstone and nephrite, the rivers, flowing lines of mercury, the vaulted ceiling a brilliant blue picked out in silver and gold.

In the chapel of the crematorium, seventeen centuries later, the older man stood with the sub-machine-gun in his hand and watched as his buyers devoured the grandeur of the terracotta creature with their eyes. He had the sub-machine-gun held lightly in the crook of his arm. He was sure of his power. He threatened no one. He merely looked at them looking. The older man said clearly and as a statement of something already settled, 'My name is Colonel Kau of the Ministry Of External Calm – the Chinese Secret Service. For the information I have in my head I wish to defect to Taiwan and then on to the United States of America.' He was speaking English. As a precursor to his new life, he was practising the language. He tapped at the terracotta armour with the knuckles of his free hand and, smiling, changed to Mandarin so there would be no doubt in the squad's minds exactly what it was he said. Colonel Kau said, 'For this, however, for this gift I have brought you, I want *money*.'

He looked up and, in an awful instant, he saw Feiffer in the loft.

They heard the shooting. In the first car, O'Yee, drawing his gun, shouted to PC Lee driving, 'Don't worry about the bloody gate – drive through it! Knock it down!' He felt the surge of power as Lee put his foot down and went for the gate. Behind the gate there was the crematorium. It was a monolith, a square grey, empty echo chamber: he heard the shattering roar of an Ingram loose off its entire magazine of thirty shots in a single burst and then, above it, through it, as another's magazine went off like a sheet of canvas being violently ripped apart, single shots from a revolver and then the hard, sharp bark of an automatic shooting rapid-fire as someone ran for cover. The wire gate came down in a tearing and twisting of metal as Lee went through. O'Yee, craning back past Yan in the back seat, saw Auden and Spencer and Miss Fan, a second behind him, take out another section of the fence with their car. He had the side door open before Lee had pulled up. O'Yee, yelling to Auden as he got out with a pump-action shotgun in his hand and chambered a round in a single action, yelled, 'There! Harry's in there!' There was a roar as an Ingram, shooting a cyclic rate of twelve hundred rounds a minute emptied its magazine, then another, then the sound of a revolver, shooting fast, and O'Yee shrieked, 'Phil, in the front door with me!' Spencer was getting out of his side of the car carrying his short-barrelled revolver. He looked at it in dismay for a moment. O'Yee shouted, 'Auden, give him your magnum!' He saw the giant gun being tossed over. O'Yee, running, moving, yelled, 'Bill, in the back! Cover the back!' He saw Miss Fan out of the car and running with Spencer, her handbag in her hand. He saw what came out. It was a silenced long-barrelled target pistol: a killer's gun. O'Yee shouted – He saw her running cocking the piece as she went, throwing the handbag to one side. She was keeping up with Spencer. She was with him, going to the back. O'Yee, hesitating only a moment, yelled to PCs Lee and Yan, 'Come on! Come on!' He yelled to Yan as he thought of it, 'The truck! Go back to the truck and shoot the tyres out!' He saw Yan nod and turn to run back towards the removal truck parked on the other side of the knocked-down wire fence. O'Yee shouted to Lee, 'You! With me!'

'Christopher!' Auden, beside him, bringing up the big gun, yelled, 'Up and down! You or me?' He meant who was to be low man and who high when they got to the door.

There wasn't any door. The door had long gone. There was only a long, dank corridor. There was a burst of shooting, not a full magazine, half: they were running, shooting in short bursts, searching. O'Yee, shaking his head, shouted above the noise, 'No, no one –' He was at the open door. O'Yee shouted, 'Down the corridor – put a round down the corridor to let them know we're here!' He ducked as Auden laid the barrel of the shotgun down the corridor and, shooting high, took out a section of the ceiling in a shower of broken laths and masonry dust and bricks. O'Yee shouted, *'Harry!'* The place was a warren of corridors and rooms and chapels. There were people running. He heard their footsteps. They seemed to be everywhere. He had no idea who the hell was in there with Kau and Feiffer. They were above him: he heard footsteps running hard on wooden floors. They seemed to be above, in the corridors and little rooms. There was a blast of fire and then an answering banging from a revolver and then he heard more people running, coming directly towards him, and then, in the echoing vaults of the place, they seemed to be running away.

There were people everywhere. O'Yee heard Spencer's voice yelling something at the far rear of the building. He heard a quick burst of fire and then two reverberating blasts from the giant magnum and then, and then – then there was a silence. O'Yee ordered Lee, 'You! Secure the entrance and don't let anyone out!'

O'Yee, racing down the long, broken corridor with Auden next to him loading buckshot rounds into the magazine of the pump-action as he went, shouted as if somehow his voice might keep him alive until they got to him, 'Harry! *HARRY!*'

16

He had killed two of them. In the first moment when they had seen him he had shot two of the soldiers and, from the way they had fallen, killed them. He had been shot. In the first moments when they had seen him the railing of the loft had exploded into splinters as a full burst from one of the Ingrams tore into it and as he ran back for the stairs, the pain came down on him like a curtain. His coat and hand and wrist were saturated in blood and as he ran he heard the shattered bones in his left elbow scrape and grind against each other. He wasn't running – he was slowing, beginning to fade. He looked down and the blood was running down from his fingers and leaving a trail. Somewhere else in the building he heard the shooting. He heard voices. Feiffer, grasping at his elbow, holding it together, his revolver becoming clogged and slippery with the blood, made for the stairs. They were coming. He heard them running.

He had come from nowhere. They had all been gazing at the statue, their guard down, and he had come from nowhere and been there watching them. All the training had been for nothing. They had not seen him. In the first exchange of gunfire all his men had shot wild and two of them had gone. By one of the bodies, the Captain, all the training gone for nothing, all of them in panic, shrieked in Mandarin, 'Up there!' His men had gone, dissipated, fled: he heard heavy shotgun rounds going off in the corridors and, from behind, more shots from a magnum. All his people were running, being killed, their training all for nothing. The Captain, looking up, seeing the Colonel with his cut-down Sterling running for a side door, yelled, 'To me! Form on me! To me! Protect the statue!' Up there in the loft there was the European: for an instant he saw his white coat covered in blood. He was moving, slowing, going around in circles, shot hard. The Captain yelled, 'To me! Form on me!'

In the front corridor O'Yee yelled, 'Phil!' They were passing doorless rooms, Auden swinging the shotgun in and covering them as they went. They were reaching the end of the corridor, going deeper into the building. O'Yee, seeing Auden going too fast, being overtaken by the approaching end, seeing the momentum carrying him too far, yelled, 'Phil, slow down! *Slow down!*' He heard a burst of gunfire from the rear of the building, coming towards him, going towards Feiffer, and O'Yee, gaining momentum, running past the open rooms, shrieked to Auden, hesitating, 'Go on! Don't stop! *Go on!*'

He was coming. She saw him. He had turned down one of the corridors and he was coming, pulling at the bolt on his Ingram. He was Chinese: a soldier. He was no soldier at all. She saw his eyes wide with terror. Miss Fan, dropping to one knee and aiming the long-barrelled target pistol, shouted to Spencer in front and to one side of her, 'Drop!' She saw Spencer turn and see the man coming at him. She heard the click as the bolt on the Ingram came back and the man's fingers reached for the butt and the trigger. Miss Fan, drawing a bead between the running man's eyes and holding the front sight on it as he came, shouted, 'Drop! I've got him! Drop!' They were not trained, the police. They were plodders, believers in life. Miss Fan, seeing the Ingram come up, yelled as Spencer turned with the magnum in his hand, 'Do what you're –' She was shouting in Mandarin. He didn't understand a word of what she was saying. Miss Fan said – She saw Spencer spin around with the big gun going up and then the man, running into it, disintegrate in a blast that shattered at the roof and brought laths and masonry down. Spencer yelled, 'Come on!' He didn't check the soldier. The soldier was dead. Spencer, coming back and taking her by the arm as if she was a helpless, panicked woman, yelled at her in Cantonese, 'Come on! Don't stay there! You're not safe! Stay with me!' He had taken the top of the running soldier's head off. He ran through the blood, pulling her by the wrist. All through the building there was the sound of shooting. Spencer, turning for a second, strengthening her with a look, said, 'Come on! Come on!'

He had lost the stairs. He had come up to the loft from the ground floor by metal stairs, but they were gone. His eyes were blurring. The pain was starting and blurring his eyes and he could not find the metal stairs. He was going in circles, slowing down, trying to find something. He had forgotten what. The gun in his hand was increasing in weight, the blood dripping from his left elbow had somehow got all over the gun he held in his right hand, and he could not find the stairs to get out. They were coming. His hearing was going. He heard buzzing sounds and then, somewhere, shots, explosions, running. He tried to find the stairs, but they were gone. He saw blackness, blurs, silhouettes, nothing. Feiffer, swimming in pools of pain, reached out and felt hard metal on his hand. He found the stairs.

He began going upwards to the room above the loft. Up there, there was no way out. He felt tears running down his face. It seemed such a pity. He could only find the stairs going up. They were the wrong ones. They were the only ones he could find.

Slowly, a step at a time, he began climbing.

O'Yee shouted, 'Harry!' They had reached the centre rooms. The layout was corridors leading onto central rooms and then more corridors leading off again into more rooms. They were in an empty, grey room where the people congregated for funerals. He saw the stained glass. O'Yee, standing in the centre of the room under a circular domed skylight, yelled at the top of his voice, '*Harry!*' He saw Auden moving from one door to the other, swinging the shotgun down the empty corridors. He heard, a long way away, Spencer's magnum and then, filling his lungs with air to shout, O'Yee yelled –

O'Yee yelled, 'Phil –!' He saw one of the soldiers. He saw
Auden at the next corridor. He saw the soldier as a shadow.
O'Yee, twisting, hitting the floor as the man came out with his
bloody awful cannon or machine gun or whatever it was,
yelled, '*Phil!*' He saw Auden come out from the corridor. He
saw the shadow turn into an armed man. He saw the Ingram
come up. He saw the look on Auden's face. He saw the shotgun
moving. He heard a click. It was either Auden's gun jamming
or the catch on the Ingram. He heard the soldier say something. He saw – The floor around him exploded in a burst of
gunfire and destruction and O'Yee went over and over, rolling,
racing the line of bullets, the revolver in his hand flying away
and falling, hitting the ground and bouncing. He heard a click.
It was Auden clearing the gun. He heard a click. It was the
Ingram. The soldier was shaking, pulling at it, putting a new
magazine into the receiver. He saw Auden running towards
him. He seemed to be a long way away. O'Yee, rolling over
and over, back for his gun, shaking his head, yelled –

O'Yee said, 'Oh my God –' He saw the Ingram come up. It
fired thirty rounds so fast that it came out as a single echoing
blast. O'Yee, dodging, rolling, going backwards and forwards
like a terrified animal as the shots sprayed wild, thought over
and over, 'Oh my God! Oh my God!' He saw the man come
out with another magazine. He saw Auden. Auden was standing there watching him. It was taking minutes. It was taking
fractions of a second. O'Yee, on the point of death, yelled,
'Phil –' He saw the soldier disappear in a haze of what looked
like fine dust. He saw the Ingram fly out of his hand. He saw
the soldier, as the dust around him settled, look surprised. He
saw him look to Auden.

The second blast from Auden's shotgun, fired a thousandth
of a second after the first – all the things happened at once –
took him full in the chest and knocked him over. He heard
Auden yell, 'OK? *OK?*'

He was getting up. He was getting up reaching for his gun.
O'Yee, shaking his head, yelled, 'OK! *OK?*'

*

He was shrieking in Mandarin. The driver, pulling at the Colonel's sleeve as he ran, shrieked in Mandarin, 'You did this! You!' They were all dead, all his friends, his comrades: all of them. The driver, hanging on, pulling as the Colonel ran down a corridor to safety, holding him back, wrenching at him, shrieked, 'You! This is your work! This is a Communist trick!' He was being dragged. He was not going to let go. The driver, dead weight on the man, holding him back, trying to get his Ingram up to cut the man's spine in half, shrieked like a child hanging onto his mother's skirts, 'You! You did this!' The driver, pulling, shouting, trying to get the Ingram up with one hand and work the safety catch, his eyes full of tears, yelled in accusation, 'I only wanted to go home!' He felt the Colonel turn and try to push him away. He hung on. He dragged, pulling the man down. The driver, pushing the receiver of the Ingram hard against his own chest so as to in some way force the safety catch off, yelled, 'No! You're not getting home! *No!*' He heard the Captain shouting as he ran towards him. He was somewhere close. The driver, dragging, pulling the man down, braking him, shouted, 'Sir! Sir! Here! He's here!' He saw the shortened Sterling in the Colonel's hand seem to go up to-wards his face. He heard a click. He saw the Colonel's hands, flailing around as he was dragged back, slam something black and rectangular into the gun and the driver, with only seconds to live, yelled, 'Captain! Captain! *Here!*' He let go. He was afraid of letting the man escape and he grabbed for him again. The Ingram was against his chest: he could not get the catch to work. He saw the Colonel turning. He was free. He saw his eyes. He saw what was in them.

The driver, on the point of death, in the last moments of his life, trying to be a good soldier, hanging on no longer to the Colonel, but to the one identity in his life, to the one thing he had ever believed in, to the one person who had ever given him warmth and a sense of belonging, yelled, 'Captain, moving to the rear! He's moving to the rear!' He saw the muzzle of the Sterling come up. He thought for a moment the squad were all together again. He thought they were at the airport going home. He thought for a moment the Captain, smiling, put his arm around his shoulders and congratulated him. He thought –

Kau, slipping the selector switch on the Sterling to Repetition, touched off a single shot and swatted him like a fly.

He began to run back towards the chapel.

'Harry!' He heard him. It was O'Yee. Feiffer, climbing higher up the stairs, going nowhere, seeing no end to it, shaking his head, said, 'Yes!' He said it as if O'Yee was beside him. He heard a buzzing. He felt moisture all down his arm and around his feet. It was his own blood. He was a void, a hole, a darkness – going forever upwards.

'Harry –!'

Feiffer, going, falling, slowing, drifting away, said, 'Yes . . .' He thought, from a long time ago in Shanghai when he had been a boy, he heard someone calling. It was a uniform: a policeman – his father. He saw on his chest the uniform and the badges of the Shanghai International Police. He thought for a moment he saw his father's eyes. He saw them as in a mirror. They were his own: grey and tired. He thought for a moment– He heard clattering behind him, boots, like his father's clambering up behind him, then running, then slowing down, inevitable, and he thought – He was going nowhere. All the blood and strength was leaking away from him and when he turned back on the stairs to look all he could see was blackness.

He heard a voice.

The voice said in Mandarin with a terrible edge to it, 'All my people are dead.' It was coming from a long way away. It was the voice of the man in charge of the soldiers. The voice, coming closer, not behind but ahead of him – no, behind – *somewhere*, said again, 'All my people are dead.' He saw a shadow. His hand touched something. His gun was gone. His hand touched something and it was the shattered and splintered railing of the organ loft and he had gone around in a complete circle and gone up the stairs and somehow come down again and, in the darkness and ebbing of life, he had – He saw a shadow in front of him.

It was the Captain.

The Captain, at the railing of the organ loft, shrieked at him in Mandarin, 'All my people are dead!' He had a square black automatic pistol in his hand.

He brought it up to kill.

'Don't kill him!' They were in the chapel at the statue. Miss Fan, knocking Spencer's gun out of his hand and getting in front of him with the Hi-Standard pistol up, yelled in English, 'Don't kill him! He has diplomatic immunity and so do I!' He was there, in front of her, at the statue, the Sterling jammed and useless in his hand. Miss Fan, advancing on him, the barrel of the silenced gun going for his neck, shaking her head, said over and over, 'No, you mustn't kill him —' Miss Fan, moving, going forward, said over and over, her voice dropping, getting tighter, 'No . . . no . . . no . . .' Miss Fan said with breathlessness, 'No, it mustn't be you . . .'

The gun was in his hand. The Captain, putting it carefully on the railing, his eyes on Feiffer, said in a whisper, 'No . . .' His eyes had glazed and gone dull. He had his hands up together in front of his chest in an attitude of prayer. He wore black gloves. He put his left hand to his right and, a finger at a time as he came towards Feiffer, began pulling the glove off.

The Captain, smiling thinly, raised his hand and made of it a fist with the second joint of the second finger protruding out in a little triangle to form a killing edge.

The Captain, moving closer, concentrating all his power and strength into his hand, said softly, coaxingly, 'Everything . . . all my people . . . all my stupid, poor, dumb people . . .' He came closer and closer through a paroxysm of pain and blackness at Feiffer's eyes. He was a blur. He was death.

The Captain, his voice dropping like a lover's, said softly, 'You . . . you have killed all my poor, stupid people . . .'

'Christopher —!'

O'Yee yelled, 'No!' He saw the gun pressed hard against Kau's neck. By him, was the wonderful statue. O'Yee halted, stopped, his gun up, yelled at the top of his voice, 'Kill him and I'll empty my bloody gun into the fucking statue!' He saw

Spencer a little behind her on the floor reaching down for Auden's magnum. O'Yee yelled, 'The statue! Bill – if she shoots –'

'Even Thoreau, Christopher – even Thoreau –!' She had the gun hard against Kau's neck for the execution shot. Miss Fan, shaking her head, said in English with her eyes glittering, 'Know your dates! Thoreau – your man of retreat and escape from the world – lived in a period of peace! He died in 1862, in the first years of the American Civil War. The American Civil War would have engulfed him!' Kau had his eyes closed. He knew what was coming. 'We are all engulfed!' She saw the muzzle of O'Yee's weapon pointed past her at the Emperor who had waited almost seventeen hundred years solely for her. Miss Fan shouted, 'Kau is my uncle! He is the man who raised me!' She was pushing the gun down onto him as if somehow without shooting him, she could stab him with it. Miss Fan, shaking her head, knowing no one understood, shouted, 'You and I and he are unimportant! It is the life of a nation that goes on!'

O'Yee ordered Spencer, 'Shoot the damned –'

Miss Fan shrieked, '*No!*'

'Bill, shoot the damned statue!'

Miss Fan shrieked, '*NO!*'

He was there. His father was there. He had come up the stairs in their apartment in Shanghai to say goodnight to him and his father was there. He saw him. He was a huge man: to a child enormous – a giant with soft grey eyes and strong hands and a voice that to a child –

The Captain, reaching him, said as a lover, 'All my hopes and plans . . . I tried so hard to get them all home, but they were . . .' He sighed. He had his hand made into the fist drawn back against his side and he sighed as he gathered strength into it for the blow. The Captain, making a hissing sound, said –

He was there. He saw him. He was there. Feiffer, trying to clear his eyes, feeling his life dripping away with the blood, going, losing consciousness, said, 'There? Are you –' He thought for a moment of his wife's face – He thought – Hong Kong, China, everything he had ever known or thought of or wanted to be was changing and going and he – and his father was coming up the stairs again as he had done every night in Shanghai and he was –

Feiffer, trying to draw himself up as he sank away, as he drifted, said in Shanghainese, 'I – I just wanted to . . .'

Auden said softly from the doorway to the organ loft, 'Hey!' He saw the Captain's eyes and the way he held his fist and for once, he needed no Spencer to explain to him what was happening in the world and what he should think about it. Auden said softly, 'Hey . . .'

He saw Feiffer's face.

The Captain turned full on to face him and Auden, with a single shot from the pump action, killed him where he stood. Auden, going towards Feiffer, said softly, 'Hey . . .'

'No!' She thought the shot was Spencer's. Miss Fan, throwing the gun down hard on the floor in front of the statue as if it was red hot, shouted, 'No.' She saw O'Yee's face.

O'Yee ordered Spencer, 'Take them!' He saw Spencer go forward to get the gun and the jammed Sterling. O'Yee said decisively, 'No, no, this is still Hong Kong!'

For the first time, he looked full on at the statue.

Was it?

It was China.

It had always been China.

O'Yee said in a gasp of wonderment, 'Christ Almighty . . . !' He saw Miss Fan's face.

For a moment, he almost wanted to say he was sorry to her.

In the loft Feiffer said softly, 'Phil. It's you . . .' It seemed too much to understand. Feiffer, looking puzzled, said quietly, 'I thought it was someone else . . .'

Auden said, hurt, 'Oh –' He leaned down with a wadded handkerchief to stop the bleeding from Feiffer's arm.

Feiffer, smiling at him, said with pleasure, 'But I'm really – honestly –' Feiffer, smiling wonderfully at him, said, putting his good hand on the man's shoulder, 'I'm really glad it was you.'

Auden said, 'Oh.' It was the nicest thing anyone had said to him in days. Auden, grinning, said, 'Oh.' Auden said happily, 'You know me, Boss, always ready to help my fellow man.' He pushed too hard with the wad and Feiffer said in pain, '*Oh!*'

Well, at least there wasn't a fire bucket in the place. Auden, pressing so gently that it hardly did any good at all, said, 'Don't worry. You'll be all right.' He tried to lift the man up, but wounded, with no strength of his own to help, he was too heavy.

Auden, sighing, said with resignation, 'Don't worry, I'll get Spencer up here to help.'

He looked at the object in front of him in the chapel and neither he nor Thoreau had ever had the words.

He saw Miss Fan still looking at him.

O'Yee, hearing Auden calling down from the loft, ordered Spencer, 'Go up and help.' He called up to Auden, 'Is Harry all right?'

Auden yelled down, 'Yes!'

He looked at the thing that was China and then to Miss Fan. O'Yee was a Eurasian, born in San Francisco, the product of a Chinese father and an Irish mother.

It was a statue. It was nothing more. It was not China. O'Yee and all the people like him were China.

It was nothing more than terracotta and paint and glaze. In the light from the stained glass windows it shimmered.

In thirteen years Hong Kong would go back to the Chinese. At that moment it seemed like a very long time indeed.

O'Yee said softly to Miss Fan, 'I'm sorry.' He had no idea what his apology was predicated on, nor why, at the time, it was all he could think to say.

He saw PCs Lee and Yan coming in from the corridors from the front and rear of the building and, nodding to them to take Miss Fan and Kau out to the car, seeing the looks on their faces as they saw the statue, O'Yee, doing what he thought was the only thing at the time that meant anything at all, went towards the stairs to the organ loft to help Auden and Spencer assist Feiffer out to the car.

The statue, in the stained glass light, shimmered and glittered with life.

It had no life.

It was only clay and paint.

O'Yee, turning his back on it and knowing he would never see it again, went quickly and did not, for a long time, think of it again.

17

'Kwantung province.' The Jellyfish Man, in John Yin's office, his hair all grown back, said, glancing around the room, 'I'm an illegal. I swam here from China.'

'Ah.' John Yin said, 'The Society For Neglected Bones makes no distinction between illegals and legals. All we are concerned with is eternity.'

'Hmm.' The Jellyfish Man, leaning a little forward in his chair, considering it, putting his chin in his hand, and, nodding sagely, said, 'Oh.' The Jellyfish Man said politely, shrugging, 'I don't want to hurt your feelings, but I'm not really interested much in death at the moment.' He was looking good. The Jellyfish Man said, 'Hong Kong really is the land of opportunity. I've only been here two weeks and already I've landed a good job with prospects and I've managed to save eighteen per cent of my first two pay packets and it looks like I might be able to do better next week.' He saw John Yin look puzzled.

The Jellyfish Man said, 'I heard you're a good and honest man in your work here with the Society.' He leaned forward a little and narrowed his eyes.

The Jellyfish Man said conspiratorially, one Chinese to another, 'No, what I was thinking – in this nice stable little British colony you people have here . . .' He dropped his voice.

The Jellyfish Man said coaxingly, on his way up, 'I believe

185

you're also in the land business. Maybe you could sell me a nice little bit of solid real estate somewhere . . . ? Away from the harbour?'